Learning
AutoCAD 2014
with 100 practical exercises

Learning
AutoCAD 2014
with 100 practical exercises

Learning AutoCAD 2014 with 100 practical exercises

Copyright © 2014 MEDIAactive

First edition: June 2014

Published by © MCB Press, owned by Marcombo

Distributed in USA and Canada by ATLAS BOOKS, 30 Amberwood Parkway, Ash-land, Ohio 44805. To contact a representative, please e-mail us at order@bookmasters.com.

Distributed in Europe by MCB Press. To contact a representative, please contact us at info@mcb-press.com, Facebook or Twitter.

www.mcb-press.com

Cover Designer: NDENU

ISBN: 978-84-267-1985-0

Printed in EU

Introduction

LEARNING AUTOCAD 2014 WITH 100 PRACTICAL EXERCISES

These 100 exercises are designed to guide the reader through the main functions of this program. Even though it is impossible to include all the features of AutoCAD 2014 in these pages, we have chosen the most interesting and often used ones. After completing the 100 exercises in this manual, the reader will be able to use the program with ease and design objects and spaces, at both the professional and amateur levels.

THE LEARNING METHOD

Our experience in the field of education has led us to design this kind of manual in which you complete each of the program's functions by carrying out a practical exercise. Each exercise is explained step-by-step and keystroke-by-keystroke, leaving no doubt as to how each exercise must be carried out. Furthermore, we have illustrated it with descriptive images of the most important steps or the results that should be obtained, and include IMPORTANT boxes that offer additional information on the subjects treated in each exercise.

Thanks to this system, we can guarantee that, after carrying out all 100 exercises in this book, the user will be able to use the main tools in AutoCAD 2014 comfortably.

THE NECESSARY FILES

If you want to use the example files in this book, you can download them from the download section on Marcombo's website (www.marcombo.com), using the specific page in this book.

WHO SHOULD READ THIS BOOK

If you are a beginner using and working with AutoCAD, you will find a complete tour of its main functions in these pages. However, if you are an expert at using this program, you will also find this book useful to learn about the improvements in this version or to review specific functions you can find in the index.

Each exercise is treated independently, so it isn't necessary to complete them in order (even though we recommend it, as we have attempted to group exercises around common subjects). Thus, if you need to find out about something in particular, you can go directly to the specific exercise on the subject and complete it on your own AutoCAD drawing.

AUTOCAD 2014

AutoCAD is currently one of the most respected and widespread applications among designers, engineers, and architects. This version of the program contains interesting new features. Among the new interface-related features, AutoCAD 2014 offers new file tabs that make it easier to switch between open drawings, and assist in creating and opening new drawings. Command line search options are improved by automatic correction, synonym suggestion, and the hability to search different types of content by name. In terms of functions, a command is added to include aerial images with geographic location in the drawing. New point cloud formats are created. Furthermore, this version offers new Autodesk Exchange applications such as file importing from SketchUp. Autodesk 360, Autodesk's connection to the cloud, now allows users to share files and messages faster and more easily. In terms of drawing, improvements are also offered in the development of different commands (arc, join, chamfer...) and in layer management. All these new and improved features are geared toward facilitating, assisting, and speeding up the complex design process.

How *Learning* books work

The title of each exercise explains very clearly what it is about. Thus, if you are interested, you can access the action you wish to learn or review directly.

The exercises are written systematically and step-by-step, so that you can't get lost while doing them.

The number on the right-hand side of the page clearly indicates which exercise you are working on.

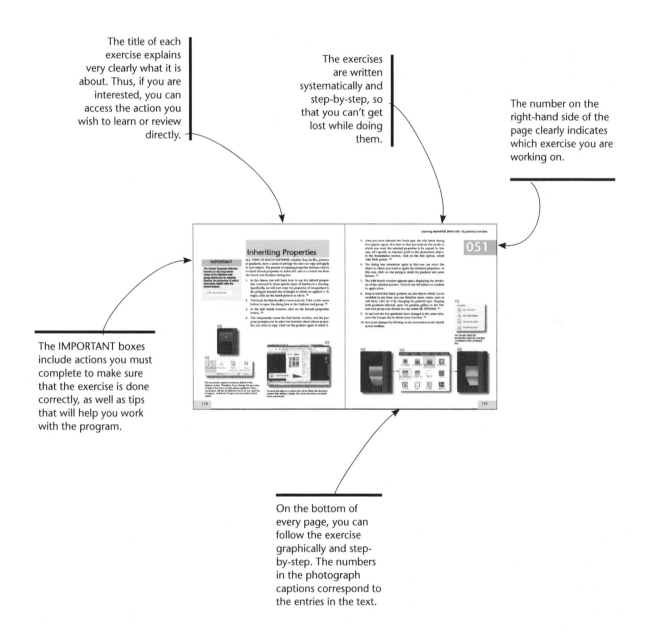

The IMPORTANT boxes include actions you must complete to make sure that the exercise is done correctly, as well as tips that will help you work with the program.

On the bottom of every page, you can follow the exercise graphically and step-by-step. The numbers in the photograph captions correspond to the entries in the text.

Table of contents

Table of contents

Starting AutoCAD 2014

EVEN THOUGH THERE IS NOTHING new to opening AutoCAD 2014 *per se*, the Welcome Screen, from which the user can access different online information sources on tools and new features for this version of the program, is a new addition.

1. A shortcut is added to your desktop during the AutoCAD 2014 install process. Double-click on this shortcut  and wait for the application to open.

2. The program will then open, displaying the new Welcome Screen from which you can access several introductory videos about the new features included in this version of the program as well as other online information about its many tools. As an example, click on the **Tour the User Interface** video.

3. Once you are done watching the video 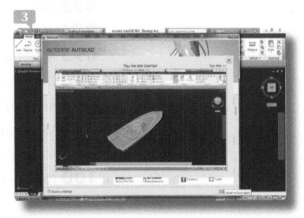 on the user interface, return to the Welcome Screen to see what other Help options are available.

4. AutoCAD 2014's Welcome Screen provides access to new or recently used AutoCAD files, and it displays the **Autodesk**

Don't forget to turn your **speakers** on or put on your **earphones** to listen to the video's explanations.

001

Exchange Apps window that allows you to download on-line resources, **Autodesk 360**, Autodesk's cloud connection, as well as Facebook and Twitter connectivity.

5. You can access the user Help section, from where you can search for different available subjects, by pressing the F1 key.

6. In the next window you can search by keyword for specific subjects, browse the Help section by following different links, and even install offline Help to store it on your computer and access it at any time. Click on the AutoCAD 2014 Offline Help link and, in the next screen, download it to the Autodesk page.

7. Proceed with the installation as in the illustration.

8. You now have access to the Help section at any time without needing an Internet connection. Close the browser by clicking the X button in its Title Bar.

9. Turn the **Display at startup** option off so that Autodesk Exchange does not appear every time you open AutoCAD, and close the window by clicking the Close button to finish this exercise.

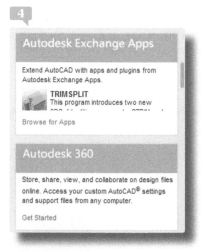

Browse the information found in **Autodesk Exchange Apps** and **Autodesk 360** on your own to learn about the new functions in AutoCAD 2014.

The User Interface in AutoCAD 2014 (I)

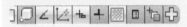
THE INTERFACE IN AUTOCAD 2014 is not markedly different from the one in previous versions. The current version is still mostly based on the Options Ribbon, which was introduced in AutoCAD 2009, and the best way to organize commands, tools, and tasks according to their usefulness in the program.

1. The **Quick Access Toolbar** is located in the upper left-hand side of the **Title Bar**, next to the workspace select command, and it displays seven tools by default: New, Open, Save, Save As, Plot, Undo, and Redo. For example, click on the third command, which is Save.

2. This opens the Save Drawing As dialog box, in which you need to enter a name and select the location for this file. Close this window by pressing the **Cancel** button.

3. Throughout this book, you will notice that all the actions you complete in this program are reflected in the **Command Line**, on the bottom part of the program's interface. In this case, merely clicking on the **Save** command reflects it as **_QSAVE** in this space. Now, float the cursor over the same command in the **Quick Access Toolbar** and notice that a tooltip appears.

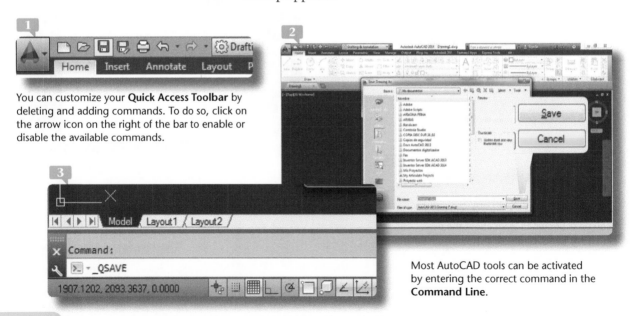

You can customize your **Quick Access Toolbar** by deleting and adding commands. To do so, click on the arrow icon on the right of the bar to enable or disable the available commands.

Most AutoCAD tools can be activated by entering the correct command in the **Command Line**.

4. This tooltip tells you which command you should type into the Command Line and a description of the command's action per se. ⬛ Try it. Click on the Command Line, type in the **Save** command, ⬛ and press **Return**.

5. The **Save Drawing As** window opens again. Close this window to continue.

6. Left of the **Quick Access Toolbar** you can find the **Application menu,** ⬛ which you will learn about in the next exercise. On the right part of the **Title Bar**, is the **InfoCenter** toolbar, from where you can conduct Help searches as well as access **Autodesk 360** and full online help with **Autodesk Exchange.** Click on the command that looks like a question mark. ⬛

7. This opens AutoCAD Help, an application you already saw in the previous exercise. Close this window by clicking on the X button in its **Title Bar**.

8. The three buttons on the right of the **Title Bar** are the usual buttons used to minimize, maximize/restore, and close buttons. Click on the X button in AutoCAD's **Title Bar** to close the application and open it again by double-clicking on its Desktop icon.

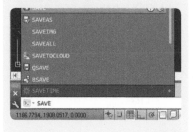

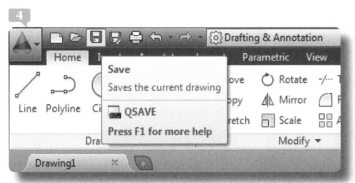

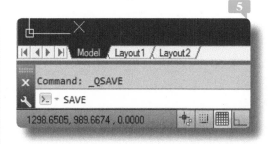

You can disable **Tooltips** from the Display tab in AutoCAD's Options dialog box.

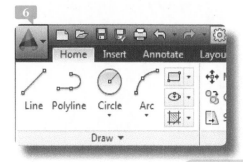

The User Interface in AutoCAD 2014 (II)

IMPORTANT

You can use the Undock option in its pop-up menu to change the Options Ribbon to a vertical position. Undocking the bar, and placing it on the left or the right, allows you to save working space. To return it to its original position beneath the Title Bar, simply drag it back there.

✓ Show Panel Titles

Undock

Close

YOU CAN HIDE AUTOCAD'S OPTIONS Ribbon so that only the titles are displayed, freeing up more space in the workspace; you can also move it to the bottom of the screen, place it vertically on one side, or let it remain floating wherever you like. You can also change the order in which the tabs appear by using the appropriate options in its pop-up menu.

1. The **Options Ribbon** is a series of tabs divided into tool groups. To move through the tabs, simply click on them. For example, click on the **Insert** tab.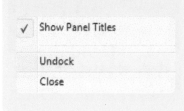

2. The arrow next to the titles of some tool groups in the Ribbon indicates that they contain more options. To only display the tabs in the Ribbon, click on the down-pointing arrow next to the Online tab and click on the **Minimize to Tabs** option.

3. Only tabs in the Ribbon are displayed. You can click on them to view their contents. To return to the Ribbon's original state, double-click on any tab.

4. As you may remember from the previous exercise, when you hover the mouse over any command in the Options Ribbon,

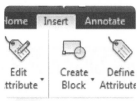

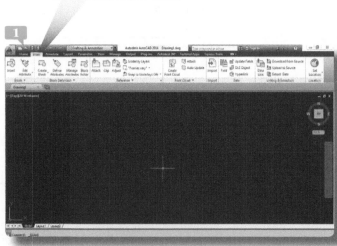

by default, the program will open a tooltip that displays the command's name, description, and equivalent path for the Command Line. If you hold this position for a few seconds, the tooltip expands to display a graphic example of the effects of this command. You can check it by hovering the cursor over the **Link** tool in the **Insert** tab, for example.

5. Most of the interface is taken up by the workspace or drawing window. This zone displays a background grid similar to graph paper to help you create your projects more precisely. There are three tabs on the lower left part of this window that you can use to change the drawing display modes. **Model** mode is used usually and by default. On the lower right part of the drawing window you can see the **Navigation bar**, which you will use several times throughout this book, as well as the **ViewCube**, located on top of the previous bar. All these tools allow you to navigate through the drawing and change the point of view and perspective from which you are looking at it.

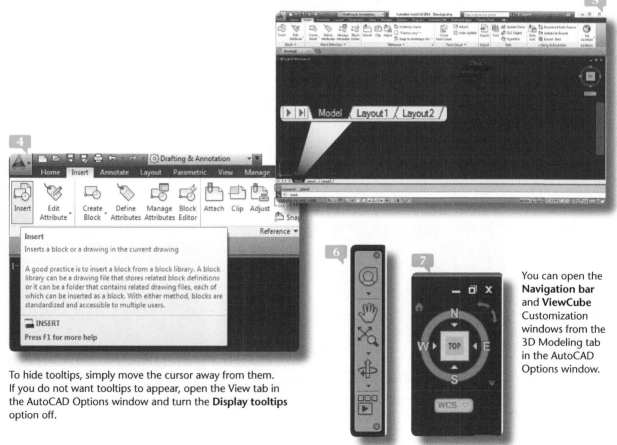

To hide tooltips, simply move the cursor away from them. If you do not want tooltips to appear, open the View tab in the AutoCAD Options window and turn the **Display tooltips** option off.

You can open the **Navigation bar** and **ViewCube** Customization windows from the 3D Modeling tab in the AutoCAD Options window.

Getting to know the Application menu

IMPORTANT

The Application menu's **Close** command includes two options: one that allows you to close the current drawing and one that allows you to close all currently open drawings.

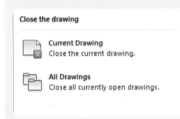

THE APPLICATION MENU IN AUTOCAD 2014 contains tools that allow you to create, open, and publish files. It has an advanced search system that allows you to find any AutoCAD command, which makes it one of the most direct and often-used parts of the program.

1. To begin, click on the icon that displays a red capital A on the left of the **Quick Access Toolbar.**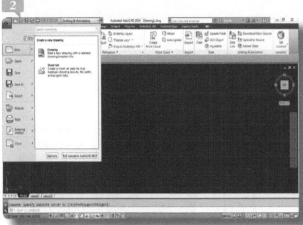

2. This opens AutoCAD 2014's Application menu. On the left is a list of commands that allow you to create, open, save, print, and publish drawings, among other actions. Each one of these main commands contains related subcommands. For example, click on the arrow on the **New** command.

3. The **New** command has two options: to create a new drawing or to create a new sheet set. Here's another example: Click on the arrow on the **Save As** command.

4. Perhaps one of the most impressive features in the Application menu is the Command Search function. Whenever you start typing in a keyword, the panel will update itself until

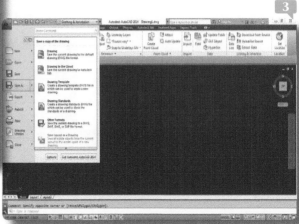

The **Application menu** contains the most commonly used file management commands.

20

004

you have obtained the desired results. Try it out: Click on the search field on the upper right-hand side of the panel and type in the word **dim**.

5. As you type, different results will appear in the panel until you find what you are looking for. Once you have found it, you can use it to run the command or function you were looking for. Before doing so, hover the cursor over the first result and wait for a few seconds until you see two tooltips appear.

6. Click on the first result, and notice how the function is run by looking at the **Command Line**.

7. As you can see, this Command Line displays that you have chosen the **_dimlinear** command. Press the **Escape** key to disable the command.

8. The two icons on the upper part of the Application menu's commands list correspond to the **Recent Documents** function, which is active by default, and the **Open Documents** function. Recent Documents are the last documents you opened with the program, whereas Open Documents gives you a list of documents that are currently being used in the program. To finish, click on a free part of the workspace to hide the Application menu.

IMPORTANT

You can see information and a **preview** of files in the Recent Documents and Open Documents lists by floating the cursor over their names.

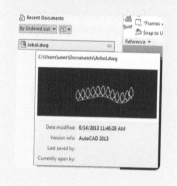

dimension

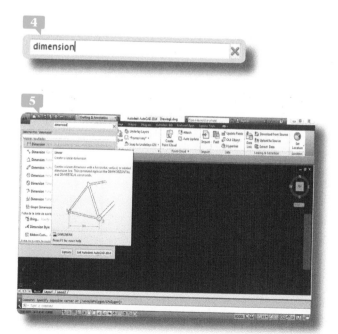

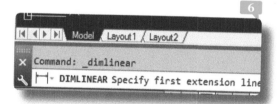

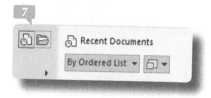

You can **organize** Recent Documents in the Application menu according to different criteria as well as **display** them as small or large **icons** or as large or small **pictures**. To do so, use the two commands underneath the Recent Documents title.

Getting to know workspaces

IN AUTOCAD, ALL THE available interfaces in the program, which depend on the type of drawings you are going to create, are called workspaces. AutoCAD has four workspaces: Drafting & Annotation (default), 3D Basics, 3D Modeling, and AutoCAD Classic. All these spaces modify the Options Ribbon with the most frequently used commands, functions, and tools.

1. This exercise will take you through the AutoCAD workspaces to learn about the main differences between them. Open the Workspace field in the Quick Access Toolbar and choose the **Drafting & Annotation** space.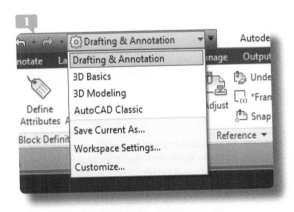

2. The **Options Ribbon** is updated to display the tools that correspond to the chosen, 2D workspace. The other items in the interface are unchanged. Click on the workspace selector again and, this time, select **3D Basics**.

3. The Options Ribbon is updated, once again, to the new space, designed for beginners in 3D modeling; its Options Ribbon combines the most common 3D modeling commands. The other items in the interface remain unchanged, which means that the Quick Access Toolbar, the InfoCenter Bar, the Command Line and the Status Bar are still available. Open the workspace selector again and select **3D Modeling**.

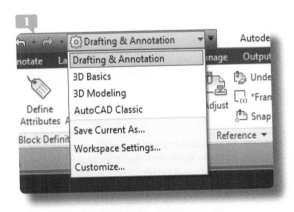

005

4. The difference between this workspace and the 3D Basics interface is obvious. For starters, the number of tabs in the Options Bar increases considerably compared to the previous one as well as the 2D drawing space; in this case, the space has 16 tabs. You should use this tab as soon as you begin to master 3D drawing. Let's have a look at the last available space. Click on the space selector again and choose **AutoCAD Classic**.

5. This workspace is like a return to the past in terms of the user interface, as the Options Ribbon gives way to the traditional tool palettes and Menu Bar. Looking at this view will make you appreciate the new Options Ribbon, which centralizes and streamlines the organization of commands. In spite of this workspace's classic appearance, the interface maintains the Quick Access Toolbar, the InfoCenter Bar and the Status Bar. Once you have looked through the workspaces available in AutoCAD 2014, return to the **Drafting & Annotation** workspace through the Quick Access Toolbar's selector or the Selection Bar now located under the toolbar.

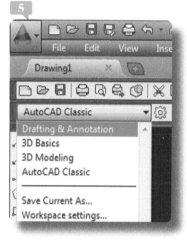

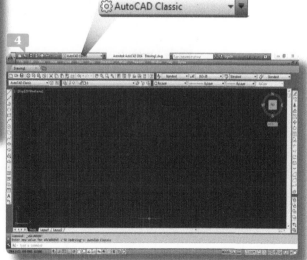

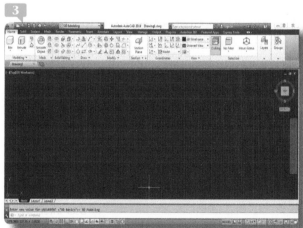

You should choose the workspace that is best suited to whatever kind of work you are performing with AutoCAD at the moment.

Customizing the workspace

AUTOCAD ALLOWS YOU TO customize any workspace so that it matches your needs. Keep in mind that customizing a workspace is only relevant when making changes to the Options Ribbon. If you change anything in the Quick Access Toolbar, for instance, those changes will also be applied to all other workspaces.

1. In this exercise we will perform a few changes in the currently active workspace, **Drawing & Annotation.** You can make changes directly on the Options Ribbon or open the interface Customization window, where you will find a large number of options to change the items it is made up of. Right-click on the **Home** tab in the Options Ribbon, click on the **Display groups** and disable, for instance, the **Annotation** group.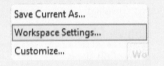

2. Notice that the **Annotation** tool group no longer appears in the Options Ribbon. This is a way of customizing the workspace. We will now see how to do so from the Customize User Interface window. Click on the workspace selector and click on the **Customize** option.

3. This opens the exhaustive **Customize User Interface** window, from which you can see and modify the item's proper-

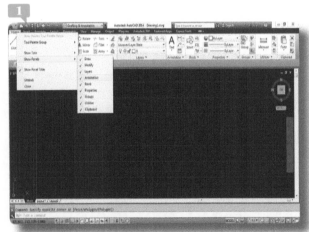

You can **hide** both tools and tabs from the Options Ribbon's pop-up menu.

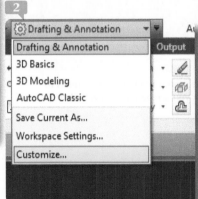

You can open the **Customize User Interface** window from the workspace selector. The suspension points next to the options indicate that a new dialog box will open when they are selected.

ties and even create new workspaces from scratch. You will now change some of the **Drawing & Annotation** workspace's features. Click on the **Customizations in All Files** panel.

4. For example, let's put the Quick Access Toolbar underneath the Options Ribbon and make the **Properties** tab always be displayed. Select the **Quick Access Toolbar 1** item in the **Workspace Contents** panel.

5. You can see the properties of the selected items in the **Properties** panel. Click on the Above Ribbon option, click on the appearing arrow and choose **Under the Options Ribbon**.

6. Now click on the + to the left of the **Palettes** item and select the **Properties** palette.

7. Open the **Display** field in the Properties panel and choose the **Yes** option.

8. Once you have set the changes, apply the new customized space by clicking on the **Apply** and **OK** buttons and look at the results.

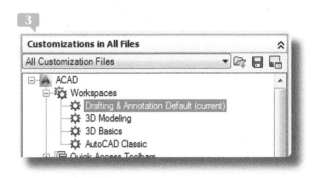

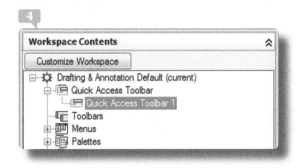

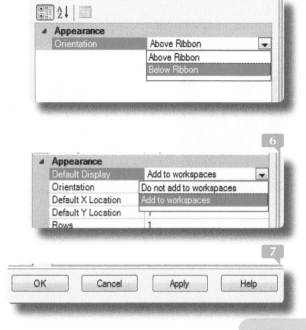

Saving workspaces

AS YOU CAN SEE, WORKSPACES control menu displays, toolbars, and palettes in the drawing area and are managed from the Customize User Interface window. Once you have customized a workspace, AutoCAD allows you to save it so you can use it again at any time.

1. Begin this exercise with your modified **Drawing & Annotation** workspace. Remember that, in the previous exercise, you changed the location of the **Quick Access Toolbar** and displayed the Properties palette. Open the Workspaces field in the **Quick Access Toolbar**, now under the Options Ribbon, and choose the **Save Current As...** option from the list.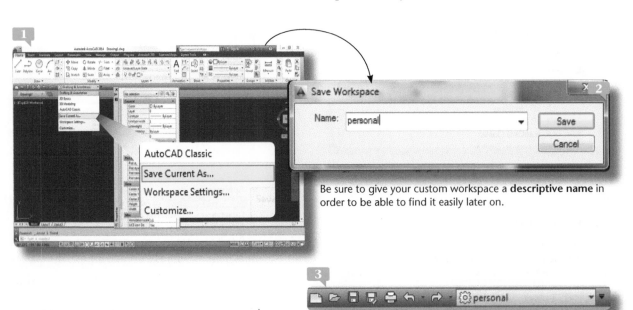

2. This opens the **Save Workspace** dialog box, in which you can assign a name to the new space. In this case, for example, type **personal** in the **Name** field and click on the **Save** button.

3. Notice that the name you chose now appears in the workspace field in the Quick Access Toolbar, since this is the currently active space. As you can see, the process of saving a custom workspace is easy. You will now see how to delete

Be sure to give your custom workspace a **descriptive name** in order to be able to find it easily later on.

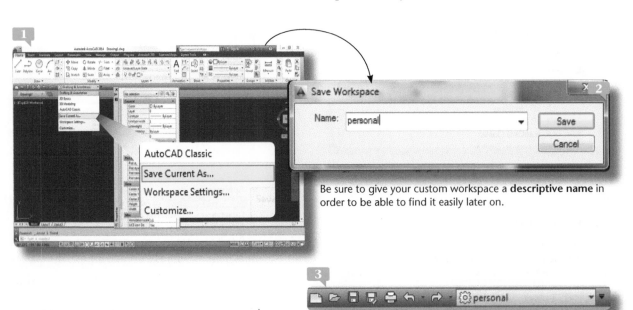

it. Click on the Workspace selector and select the **Drawing & Annotation** space.

4. Open the selector's menu again and click on the **Customize** option.

5. Notice that, in the Customizations section in All Files, the style you created is already listed. Right-click on it to open its pop-up menu.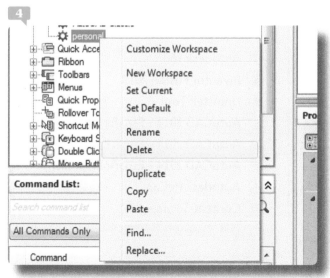

6. You can customize this space, define it as the current workspace, make it the default space, create a new space, etc., from this menu. Click on the **Delete** option.

7. Confirm that you wish to delete the personal workspace by clicking the **Yes** button in the dialog box that appears on your screen.

8. The workspaces list is updated, both in the Customization window as well as in the selector, as you will now see to finish this exercise. Click on the **Apply** and **OK** buttons in the Customization window.

9. Click the Workspace selector again and, after noticing that the **personal** workspace no longer appears in it, close the menu by clicking on the **Drawing & Annotation** space.

You can set the workspace with which AutoCAD will open by default both from this menu in the Customization window as well as from the **Workspace Settings** window.

Restoring default settings

IN THE AUTODESK FOLDER that is added to the Windows Start Menu when you install AutoCAD 2014, you will find a new tool that allows you to restore AutoCAD's settings to defaults. This is a simple and fast operation with which you can undo a migration or discard custom changes.

1. Since you modified the **Drawing & Annotation** workspace in previous exercises, you will now learn about the usefulness of **Restore Default Settings**, a new and useful AutoCAD 2014 tool that allows you to recover the program's default settings. In order to use this new feature, the program must be closed; therefore, you should click on the X button in the program's **Title Bar**.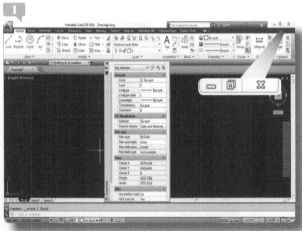

2. Open the **Start** Menu, click on the **All Programs** button, locate and open the **Autodesk** folder, and click on the **Auto-CAD 2014** subfolder.

3. Click on the **Reset Settings to Default** option.

It is also possible that you will find the **Restore Settings to Default** option in the Start Menu after installing AutoCAD.

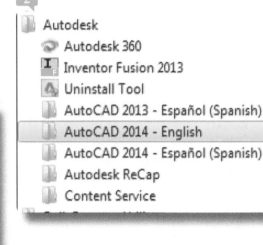

008

4. This opens the **Reset Settings – Backup** window, in which you can choose to either create a backup in ZIP format with your customized files and settings, specifying a location and a name for them, or to directly reset your settings without making a backup copy. Click on the **Backup and reset custom settings** options.

5. In the **Backup Custom Settings** window, keep the **Documents** folder selected as well as the default name and click on the **Save** button.

6. The length of time it takes to create a settings file depends on its size. During this process, a window will appear telling you that it is being carried out. Once it is done, a new window will confirm that the original AutoCAD 2014 settings have been reset correctly. Notice that the AutoCAD is back to its original state. Close the **Reset Settings – Backup** window by clicking on the **OK** button.

7. The application will then restart automatically. Disable the **Show this window at start up** option in the Autodesk Exchange window, click on the Close button, and notice that, indeed, the program interface is back to its original state.

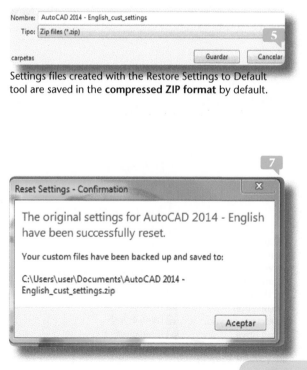

Settings files created with the Restore Settings to Default tool are saved in the **compressed ZIP format** by default.

Creating and opening documents

IMPORTANT

In order to Create New Drawings you can also open the **Create New Drawing** window by setting the **STARTUP** and **FILEDIA** variables to 1 from the Command Line. Doing so, as when running the New command from the Quick Access Toolbar or the Application menu, opens the Create New Drawing dialog box.

WHEN OPENING AUTOCAD 2014, a white drawing based on a blank template, called acadiso.dwt, is loaded into the workspace by default. Its main feature is the immediate application of a grid. However, you can choose to Create New Drawings that are not based on a template.

1. In order to create a document with the same characteristics as the default one, **Drawing1.dwg**, click on the **New** icon, the first one in the **Quick Access Toolbar**.

2. In the **Select Template** window you can see the default template, a blank template with a series of preset settings and characteristics and with the grid enabled. Click on the **Open** button to load the new blank drawing into your workspace.

3. In the Title Bar you can see that this is a new document, **Drawing2.dwg**. Close it by clicking on the X button in the upper right corner of the workspace.

4. Create a new drawing, this time from the Application menu and without using a template. Open the Application menu, click on the **New** command and choose the **Drawing** option.

AutoCAD templates are saved in the **Template** folder, in the program's installation directory on your hard drive.

To close a document, use the X button in the workspace. To close the program, use the X button in the **Title Bar**.

009

5. Back in the **Select Template** window, click on the arrow on the **Open** button and choose the **Open Without Template - Metric**.

6. In the Title Bar you can see that the new drawing has been created. At first glance the only difference with the default file is that there is no grid. However, you can enable or disable it according to your own preference. Click on the third icon in the **Status Bar**.

7. It now looks identical to the default drawing. Click on the X button on the current document's drawing area.

8. The program then displays a dialog box asking you if you wish to save the changes. Click on the **Yes** button.

9. Keep the default location in the **Save Drawing As** window, type **test** in the **Name** field, and click on the **Save** button.

10. You will see how to recover this document. To do so you can use the **Open** command in the **Quick Access Toolbar**, the same command in the Application menu, or via the Recent Documents list in that menu. Open the Application menu and click on the **test.dwg** file on the right of the panel.

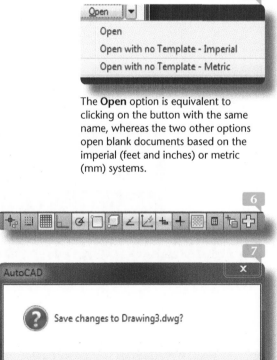

The **Open** option is equivalent to clicking on the button with the same name, whereas the two other options open blank documents based on the imperial (feet and inches) or metric (mm) systems.

The list of Recent Documents in the Application menu can be organized according to different criteria.

Configuring documents

YOU CAN CONTROL the place where AutoCAD looks for and saves files, as well as choosing how they are displayed, in the Options dialog box, which you can open from the Application menu.

1. Open the program's general Options window. Open the Application menu and click on the **Options** button.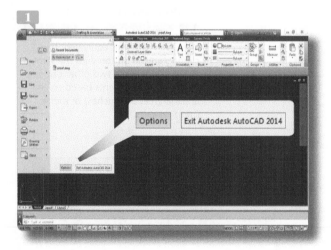

2. In the **Files** tab you can see all the necessary files and the folders where they are located; thus, you can control all files created with AutoCAD. Go to the **Files** tab and click on the + on the left of the folder called **Temporary Drawing File Location**.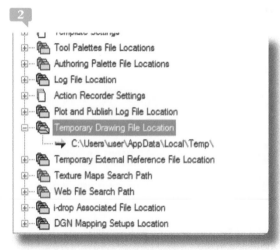

3. The program then displays the subfolders you must open to find the folder that contains temporary files of the drawings created with AutoCAD. Click on the **Display** tab.

4. In this tab you can see the necessary options to control and customize how AutoCAD 2014 is displayed as well as graphics and ways to increase the program's performance. Click on the **Colors** button in the **Window Elements** section.

To modify a subfolder, select it and open the Search for folder window via the **Browse** button.

5. You can modify the colors in most of the program's interface elements, both in the **Model** tab and in the **Display** tab, from the **Drawing Window Colors** dialog box. As you can see, the background for the 2D Model space is selected by default. Click on the arrow in the **Color** field and select **Red** from the pop-up menu.

6. You can see the change that has taken place in the Preview window. Close the **Drawing Window Colors** window without applying changes by pressing the **Cancel** button, and open the **Open and Save** tab.

7. You can specify which format files will have from this tab, how many minutes between autosaves, the number of recent files that should be listed, etc. Double-click on the **Minutes between saves** field and type **15**.

8. Click on the **Drafting** tab.

9. In this field you can establish the main settings for the **AutoSnap** marker and the **AutoSnap** marker size, among other parameters. The AutoSnap marker appears when you move the graphic cursor over a geometric symbol that displays some kind of reference. Move the sliding bar button to the right and notice how its size increases in the Preview window.

10. To finish this exercise, click on the **Apply** and **OK** buttons.

010

IMPORTANT

Logically, we cannot show you every single command included in the **Options** window, but we recommend that you experiment on your own, learning about each of their functions until you obtain the interface you like best in the program.

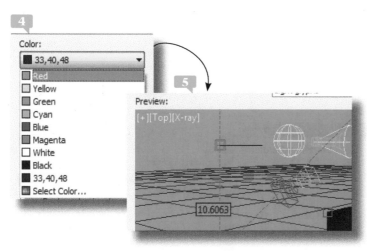

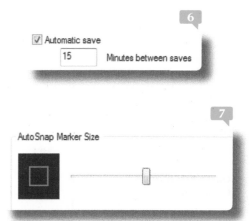

You can restore AutoCAD interface elements to their original color by clicking on the **Restore** ... buttons.

Configuring the way you create drawings

THE CREATE NEW DRAWING DIALOG BOX appears when you open a new drawing, provided that this has been enabled in the Program Options window. This dialog box displays four buttons that allow you to choose to either open a preexisting file, create a new file, open a template, or use a wizard to set advanced settings.

1. In this exercise you will see how to display the **Create New Drawing** dialog box when creating a new drawing in Auto-CAD 2014, and how to use the wizard to establish advanced settings. Type **STARTUP** in the Command Line, press the **Return** key, type 1 and press **Return** again.

2. Click on the **New** icon in the **Quick Access Toolbar**.

3. As you can see, the program displays the **Create New Drawing** dialog box, where you can choose to either open an existing drawing, open a new drawing with default settings, open a new drawing based on a template, or use a wizard to configure the new drawing. Click on the last icon in the box, **Select a Wizard**.

4. The program allows you to choose between an Advanced Setup and a Quick Setup wizard. Keep the Advanced Settings option, which is already selected in blue, and click on the **OK** button.

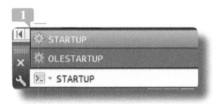

The **AutoComplete** feature in AutoCAD 2014 allows you to choose the appropiate command from a pop-up list that emerges as soon as you start typing in the Command Line.

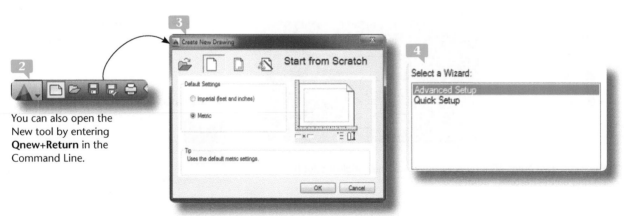

You can also open the New tool by entering **Qnew+Return** in the Command Line.

011

5. The first choice you have is to select a unit of measure and its precision. Open the **Precision** list, select the sixth type of decimal and click on the **Next** button to continue with the configuration process. 5

6. Choose the type of angle and, once again, the degree of precision. You should only change the precision of the angle. Open the list in the **Precision** field, select the 0,0 option and click on the **Next** button. 6

7. Choose the direction in which angles are measured, which is East by default. Click on the **North** button to establish that measures will be applied from the northernmost point, and click on the **Next** button.

8. In the **Angle Direction** section you can choose whether measures will be clockwise or counter-clockwise. In this case, keep the **counter-clockwise** option. Click on the **Next** button.

9. Specify which area the graphic zone will take up. Type 300 in the field that displays the drawing's width and 210 in the field that displays the length. 7

10. Once you have specified all the necessary information to create the new drawing, click on the **Finish** button.

11. A new document will be created with the specified settings. From now on, whenever you create a new drawing, the **Create New Drawing** window, in which you can choose your settings, will appear. Close the current drawing by clicking on the X button in the graphic zone.

IMPORTANT

The **Advanced Settings wizard** allows you to configure units, angles, angle measurements and directions, and the document's surface area. The small arrow that appears next to each parameter shows you the configuration phase you are currently in.

▶ Units

Angle

Angle Measure

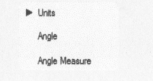

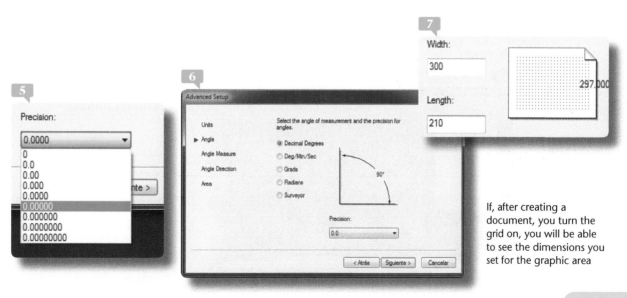

If, after creating a document, you turn the grid on, you will be able to see the dimensions you set for the graphic area

Searching with Content Explorer

THE CONTEXT EXPLORER allows you to index design contents in order to be able to access them quickly, as well as to catalog objects in drawings and search for contents in local folders, network folders, and the Autodesk Seek library.

1. In this exercise you will learn how the Content Explorer content management tool works. You can either open it from the Plug-ins tab or from the Command Line, by inserting the order **ContentExplorer + Return**. Click on the **Plug-ins** tab and click on the **Explore** command.

2. The **Content Manager** panel allows you to index and search quickly and effectively. As in all other AutoCAD secondary panels, you can change its transparency, its automatic minimization, and pinning options. Click on the third icon at the top in the panel's **Title Bar** and click on the **Transparency** option in the pop-up menu.

3. From the **Transparency** window you can change the general transparency of the palette and its appearance when you scroll the cursor over it. As you can see, you can apply settings specified in this window to all AutoCAD palettes. Move the sliding transparency button to **90%** and click on **OK**.

By default, the **Content Manager** is displayed in floating mode, but you can pin it to different parts of the area by using the options in its Settings menu.

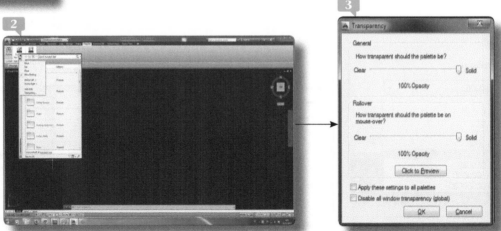

012

4. The palette is now slightly transparent until you move the cursor over it, in which case it becomes 100% opaque. Before making a simple search in the Content Manager, which only displays two inspected folders by default, **Downloaded Content** and **Sample**, let's see how to add a third folder. Click on the **Add Watched Folder** button.

5. In the **Select Watched Folder** window, find and select the folder you would like to add to carry out the search and click on the **OK** button.

6. When carrying out the search, the Content Manager will also go through your folder. Once the folder is indexed, click on the search field, enter **wall** and press the **Return** key.

7. On the lower part of the panel you can see the number of results. Notice that not only files that coincide with search criteria are listed, more contents such as blocks, layers, line styles, etc., are also included. To filter the results so that they only display layers, click on the arrow button on the Filter icon, represented by a funnel, and then only leave the **Layer** option active in the **Object Types** tab.

8. You can now save the search results, apply new filters, change the viewing mode, and even access drawings and view their properties. To finish this exercise, close the **Content Manager** by clicking on the X button in its **Title Bar**.

IMPORTANT

In order to open the Content Manager's **Settings** window, click on the wrench icon below it.

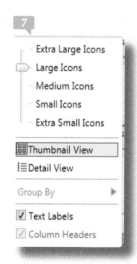

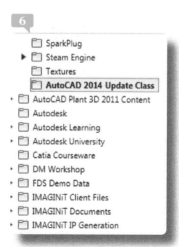

Editing a document's properties

AUTOCAD 2014 CONTAINS THE PROPERTIES tool group in the Home tab, from which you can alter many of a document's properties. This tool group consists of the most important properties of the different drawing layers.

1. In this exercise you will learn about some of the functions located in the **Layers and Properties** tool groups in the Options Ribbon. To do this you will use a sample image. Open the **Mechanical-Multileaders.dwg** drawing that is included in the **Mechanical Sample** subfolder in the main **Sample** folder of AutoCAD 2014.

2. Open the Home tab and click on the **Layer properties** icon, the first one in the **Layers** tool group.

3. The **Layer Properties Manager** is automatically displayed on-screen. It contains all the necessary information on the items that make up the drawing's different layers. Let's change the color of the items that make up the layer named **CLOUD**. Click on the black square in that layer.

4. This opens the **Select Color** window, in which you can choose the color you want to apply to the selected item. For instance, click on the first sample on the fifth row, which corresponds to red, and click on the **OK** button.

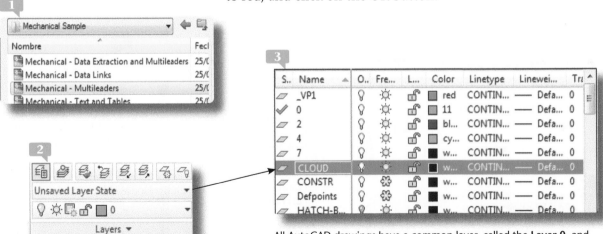

All AutoCAD drawings have a common layer, called the **Layer 0**, and, as you can see, the sample drawing is made up of several more layers, each one of them identified with a name.

5. Block all the items included in **Layer 2**. To do this, click on the icon that displays a small padlock in that layer's **Lock** column.

6. Close the Layer Properties Manager by clicking on the X button on the upper left side of its **Title Bar**.

7. You will now change the properties of the red frame that surrounds the first item in the drawing. Click on any side of this frame to select it.

8. Open the **Line Width** field, the second in the **Properties** tool group that displays the text **ByLayer**, and click on the **0.40 mm** option.

9. The change is applied correctly. To change the color of an item individually, you should access the pop-up menu in the **Object Color** field from the **Properties** tool group. Keeping the frame selected, click on the arrow button in that field, the first one in the group, and choose, for instance, **Green**.

10. A feature in AutoCAD 2014 is the property editing preview mode that allows you to get a dynamic preview of the objects before applying your changes.

11. Notice the effect of the changes by deselecting the frame (pressing the **Escape** key), and close the drawing without saving.

IMPORTANT

When selecting a part of a drawing, the **Quick Properties** panel will appear if the second to last icon in the Status Bar is active. This feature helps you increase productivity by reducing the amount of time it takes to access information on properties, optimizing viewing for a specific user or project.

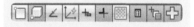

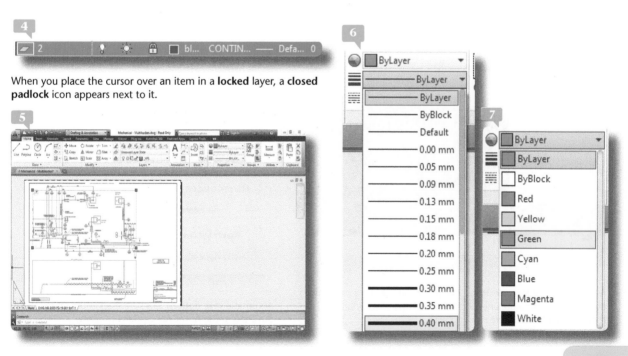

When you place the cursor over an item in a **locked** layer, a **closed padlock** icon appears next to it.

Creating and recovering backups

IMPORTANT

The **ISAVEBAK** system variable gradually improves speed when saving drawings progressively, especially when it comes to large drawings.

BACKUP FILES allow you to recover a file when problems arise from electricity failures, power surges, human errors, software or hardware failures, etc. By configuring the backup process correctly you can avoid data loss caused by such problems.

1. In this exercise you will learn which backup settings options are included in AutoCAD 2014 and how you can recover these backup copies. Let's begin the exercise by opening the **text. dwg** file you created in a previous exercise. Click on the application button and click on the **Options** command.

2. Click on the **Open and Save** tab in the **Options** window.

3. In the **File Safety Precautions** section you will notice that the Automatic save and Create backup copy with each save options are on. By default, AutoCAD will autosave every 15 minutes. To shorten this time, double-click on the **Minutes between saves field**, enter **8**, and click on the **Apply** and **OK** buttons.

4. Thus, AutoCAD will create an automatic backup of the last version you were working on, in .ac$ format, every 8 min-

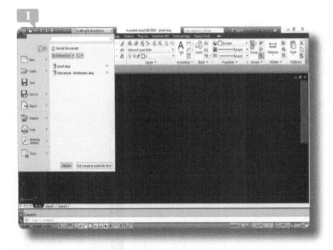

A hardware problem, electronic failure, or software bug can make the program terminate unexpectedly. **Backups** allow you to recover the files you were working with.

Automatic save options can be edited in the **Open** and **Save** tab in the AutoCAD Options window.

014

utes. Furthermore, every time you save the drawing, a back-up copy with the same name and a .bak extension, located in the same folder as the drawing file, will be generated. You will now see how to recover a backup of the **test.dwg** file, as-suming that you have already saved it and that a backup has been generated. Open the **Windows Explorer** and find the **.bak** file in question. Click on the **Windows Explorer** icon in the **Task Bar.**

5. Open the **Documents Library** by double-clicking on it and find and select the **proof.bak** backup file.

6. You can save this backup file as a **.dwg** file by changing its ex-tension without having to open it, copying it into a different folder in order to avoid overwriting the original file. Right-click on the selected item and choose the **Rename** option in the pop-up menu.

7. The file name can now be edited. Replace the name by typing **testcopy.dwg** and press the **Return** key to confirm it.

8. Confirm that you wish to change the file extension by press-ing the **Yes** button in the **Rename** field.

Finally, you can create a folder called **Backups**, for instance, and copy the new file into it so you can recover it in case you have any problems with the one you are currently working on.

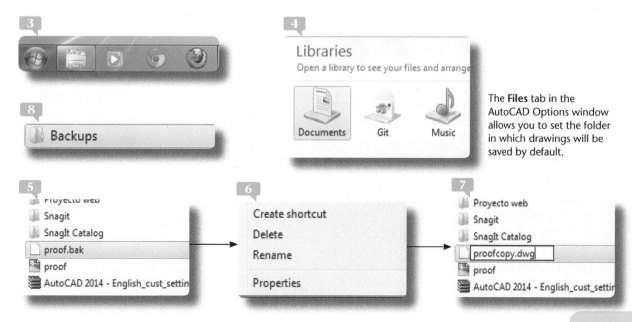

Libraries
Open a library to see your files and arrange

Documents   Git   Music

The **Files** tab in the AutoCAD Options window allows you to set the folder in which drawings will be saved by default.

Proyecto web
Snagit
SnagIt Catalog
proof.bak
proof
AutoCAD 2014 - English_cust_settin

Create shortcut
Delete
Rename
Properties

Proyecto web
Snagit
SnagIt Catalog
proofcopy.dwg
proof
AutoCAD 2014 - English_cust_settin

Backups

Working with coordinates

AUTOCAD USES A CARTESIAN (named after French philosopher René Descartes) or rectangular system of coordinates. The intersection between the horizontal and vertical axis sets the point of departure for both coordinates.

1. In this exercise you will learn how to use the coordinate system in AutoCAD. To do this, open the sample file called **Home-Space Planner.dwg**, included in the **DesignCenter** subfolder in the **Sample** folder in the program files, and change the positions of some of the items it contains. Once the drawing is in the graphics zone, ▣ click on the **Move** command in the **Modify** tool group in the Options Ribbon. ▣

2. Notice that the tooltip that appears next to the cursor, currently a small square, will tell you what to do next. ▣ In this case, you need to select which items you wish to move. Click on the piano and press the **Return** key to complete the selection.

3. Specify the base of the first point of displacement. Keep in mind tht there should be no space between the values that make up a coordinate. Type the coordinates **260,55** in the Command Line and press the **Return** key. ▣

4. The first value represents the horizontal coordinate from the X = 260 point, and the second refers to the vertical coordinate

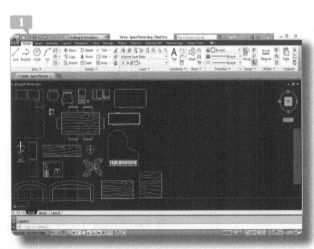

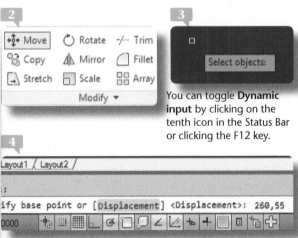

You can toggle **Dynamic input** by clicking on the tenth icon in the Status Bar or clicking the F12 key.

015

from the point Y = 55. You will now indicate the final point in the move. Depending on the move, you can enter two new coordinates that will be applied from the first ones or, as you will see in this case, you can press the **Return** key for the move to be carried out on the two set points. Press **Return** and see how the object has moved.

5. If using the Command Line is too complicated for you (as is often the case when starting out), you can move the items directly on the graphic zone by using the mouse. Here's how: First, click on the **Move** command in the **Modify** tool group again, or type in the order **_move** and press **Return** in the Command Line.

6. Click on the piano again and press the **Return** key to confirm your selection.

7. Click on the object again to specify the first point of the move and click a few centimeters to the left.

This is probably the easiest and most direct way of moving objects even though, obviously, it lacks the precision of using coordinates.

IMPORTANT

When typing values in the Command Line, **coordinates** should be separated by a comma and decimals should be specified after a dot. When a move is negative relative to the point of origin, you must include a minus (-) sign in front of the values.

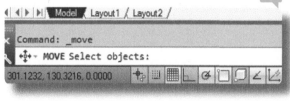

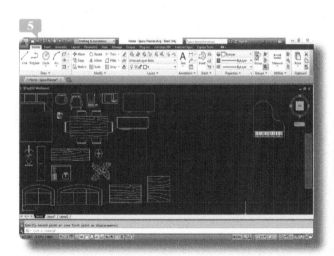

To help **moving** objects, AutoCAD keeps the selected item visible while you are locating the final point for it with the mouse.

When entering orders in the Command Line you can see that the **AutoComplete** function in AutoCAD 2014 makes your task a lot easier by providing different commands as soon as you start typing.

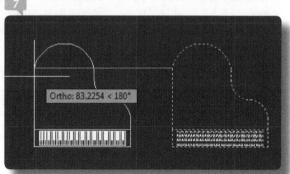

The UCS icon

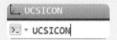
AS YOU POINTED OUT IN THE PREVIOUS EXERCISE, the UCS icon appears on the lower left corner of the work area, representing the X- and Y- axes in 2D drawings and X, Y, and Z in 3D works.

1. Depending on the workspace and visual style you are using, the UCS icon can be displayed, hidden, or modified in different ways. First, let's see how to hide the UCS icon when it is active in the **2D Wireframe** visual style. In this case, use the AutoCAD 2014 **AutoComplete** feature. Click on the Command Line, type **UCS2** and, in the list of possible commands that appears, choose the first one, **UCS2DDISPLAYSETTING**.

2. The possible values for this command are 0 to disable it and 1 to enable it. Type 0 and press the **Return** key.

3. Notice that the UCS icon has disappeared. To display it again, simply restore the value to 1. Right-click on any part of the work area and select the **Repeat UCS2DDISPLAYSETTING** option in the pop-up menu.

4. Enter 1 and press the **Return** key for the UCS icon to appear again.

5. In addition from being able to control the display of the UCS icon, you can also control its style and location from its Prop-

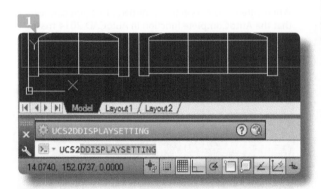

You can control the functioning of the **AutoComplete** feature from the AutoComplete command in the Command Line's pop-up menu.

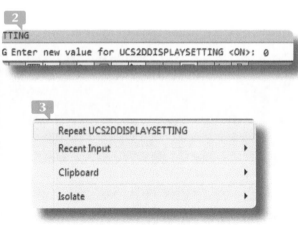

Use the **Repeat** option from the Context menu of the workspace to repeat the execution of a command.

erties window. In order to open the UCS icon's Properties window from the **Drawing & Annotation** view, right-click on it, click on the **UCS Icon Settings** option and choose the **Properties** command.

6. This opens the **UCS Icon** window, where you can view the default properties for this item. The Preview window allows you to check the results of the changes before applying them definitively. As you can see, the icon can be displayed in 2D or 3D, the default option. You will now modify the line width. Click on the **Line width** field and select **2**.

7. You can also control the size of the icon as a percentage of the size of the graphics window. By default, this is set to 50%. Double-click on the number **50** in the **UCS icon size** section and type 60.

8. In the **UCS icon color** section you can change the icon's color in the Model space and in the Layout space. You can apply a single color or different colors for each axis. Keeping the **Apply single color** option selected, open the **Layout tab icon color** field and choose, for instance, **Yellow**.

9. To apply the changes and see the resulting effect in the work area, click on the **OK** button.

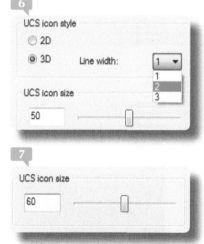

You can use the **Repeat** option in the work area's pop-up menu to carry out a command again.

The **UCS icon size** is proportional to the size of the graphics window in which it is displayed.

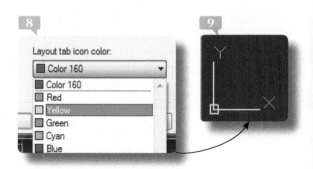

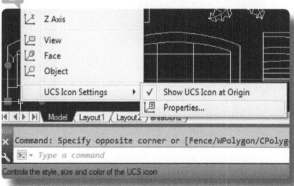

Working with relative and polar coordinates

RELATIVE COORDINATES USE coordinates relative to the last specified point whereas polar coordinates complement relative coordinates by specifying the direction of an angle you would like a specific point to take.

1. In this exercise you will learn about the difference between relative Cartesian coordinates and polar relative coordinates. To begin, select the piano in the **Home - Space Planner** sample drawing you moved in an earlier exercise by clicking on it.

2. You will now change the selected object's position by specifying a series of relative coordinates in the Command Line. Click on the **Move** tool in the **Modify** tool group.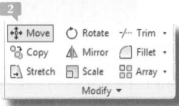

3. Type the @ symbol in the Command Line by pressing **AltGr + 2**, followed by the value **0,0**.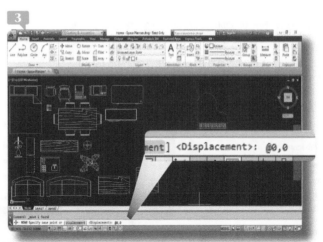

4. Press the **Return** key and specify the new point: @15,0 and press **Return** again to apply the new coordinates.

5. Notice how the object has moved horizontally. You will now specify new relative coordinates but, this time, with a nega-

Relative coordinates are distinguished by the **@ symbol** that precedes them.

tive sign in the vertical coordinate to make the object move downward. Select the object by clicking on it again.

6. We will now use a keyboard shortcut to activate the **Move** tool again. Click behind the second **Command** term in the Command Line, press the D key on your keyboard, and press the **Return** key.

7. Type **@0,-1** and press **Return** to specify the second point.

8. Type **@0,-10** and press **Return** to carry out the change.

9. Polar coordinates include relative radial distances and a horizontal-relative angle along with the new coordinates. To specify the angle, type the less than symbol (<) in front of its value. Open the Move command again and select the same object, pressing **Return** when you are done.

10. Enter the coordinates **@2<50** and press **Return** to specify that the length of the X,7 segment is 2, its direction is toward the right, and its angle is 50 degrees.

11. Specify the second point. Type @2<50 again and press **Return**.

12. To finish this exercise, press the X button in the work area and close the drawing without saving the changes.

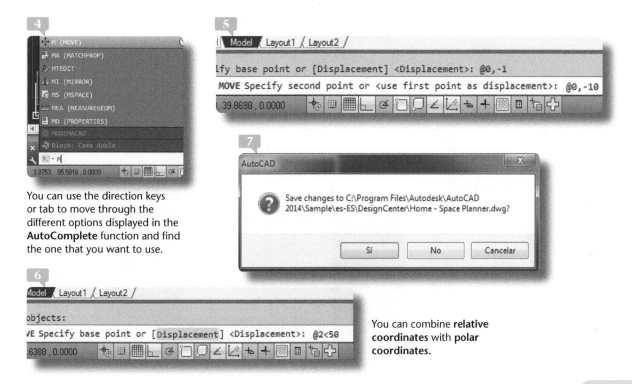

You can use the direction keys or tab to move through the different options displayed in the **AutoComplete** function and find the one that you want to use.

You can combine **relative coordinates** with **polar coordinates**.

Creating and editing layers

LAYERS ARE A BASIC organizational element in design programs such as AutoCAD, as they allow you to group information in a drawing according to its function. Layers are equivalent to the onion paper that is used when designing on paper. You can place different items in different layers to control their viewing, lock them, change their properties, etc.

1. In this exercise you will learn how to create layers in AutoCAD 2014. In this case you will work with a new document, called **First drawing**, which you may download from our website and open in AutoCAD. Throughout the following exercises you will place items that make up your sample drawing in different layers. By default, AutoCAD drawings have an initial layer, called **Layer 0**, which has specific characteristics you can see in the **Layers** tool group in the **Home** tab. In order to create a new layer, you need to access the **Layer Properties Manager**. Click on the **Layer Properties** icon, the first in the **Layers** tool group.

2. This opens the **Layer Properties Manager** palette, where you can work with layers and view their properties. In order to create a new layer, click on the **New layer** option, which apperars as a star on a piece of paper.

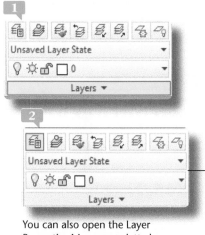

You can also open the Layer Properties Manager palette by entering the **layerpalette** command in the Command Line.

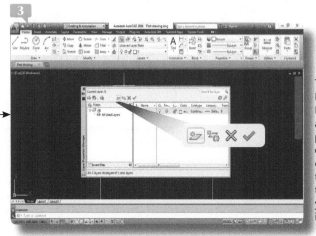

The Layer Properties Manager opens as a floating palette by default, but you can **anchor** it to any point of the work area if you drag it by its Title Bar.

018

3. A new layer automatically appears, which the program automatically names **Layer 1**, with the same properties as the original layer (color, status, type and line width, etc.). Give the new layer the name **Walls** and press the **Return** key to confirm it.

4. Keep in mind that the checkmark in the Status column will tell you which is the current layer, that is, the layer on which objects will be drawn. In this case, the current layer is still the default layer, Layer 0. In order to distinguish the objects created in the **Walls** layer clearly, you should change its color. Click on the white color sample in the **Color** column that corresponds to the new layer, **Walls**.

5. In the **Select Color** field, click on the seventh sample in the third row in the first sample group and press the **OK** button.

6. This way, whenever you draw an object on the **Walls** layer, it will have the chosen color. To finish creating and editing this new layer, you will modify the line depth as well. Click on **Default** in the **Lineweight**column that corresponds to this layer and, in the **Lineweight** window, choose the value 0.30 and click **OK**.

7. To finish this exercise, save the changes by pressing the **Save** icon in the **Quick Access Toolbar**.

As you can see, creating new layers in which to place objects is very easy. In the next exercises you will learn how to move objects from one layer to another and how to carry out other actions with these essential parts of a drawing.

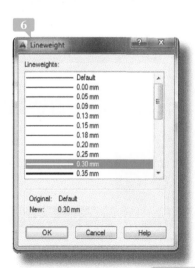

You can select one of 255 colors in the AutoCAD color index (ACI), True Colors and the ones included in the Color Books.

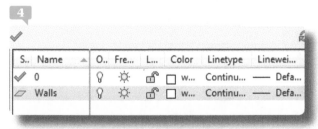

When you create new layers in AutoCAD, the program automatically names them in **numerical order** (Layer 1, Layer 2, Layer 3, etc.).

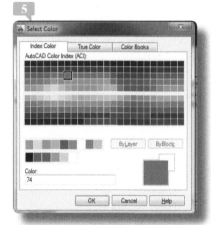

The Lineweight window displays the available line widths, made up of the most commonly used fixed values.

Moving objects from one layer to another

IMPORTANT

Not only can you move items between layers, you can also copy them. To do this, you can use the new **Copy Objects to New Layer** tool by selecting the objects you wish to copy followed by the layer in which you want to copy them.

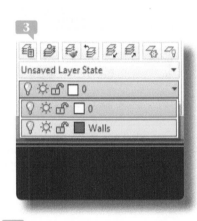

LAYERS ALLOW YOU TO CONTROL the visibility of objects and to assign them different properties. One way to keep your drawing well organized and to avoid accidental or unwanted changes is to place different types of objects or parts of the drawing in separate layers and to lock them.

1. In this exercise you will learn two different procedures for moving objects from one layer to another. Once again, you will use the **First drawing** file you saved in the previous exercise. Remember that the file has two layers, the default Layer 0 and the **Walls** layer, to which you will move the square that is drawn with lines. To begin, close the **Layer Properties Manager** palette by clicking on the X button in its **Title Bar**.

2. Objects are always created in the current layer, in this case the default Layer 0. Move one of the square's sides to the **Walls** layer by using the appropriate option in the **Layers** tool group in the **Home** tab. Click on the line on the right of the square to select it.

3. As you can see in the **Layers** group, the selected object is located in the white-colored Layer 0. Open the list of layers in the **Layers** group and choose the **Walls** layer.

4. This is perhaps the easiest and quickest way to move selections from one layer to another. Notice how the selected layer

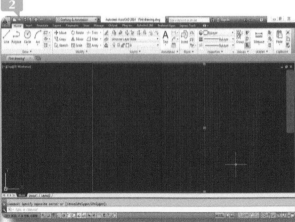

is now displayed in the green color you chose for the new layer. You will now use a second method to move the other lines into this layer. Press the **Escape** key to unselect the line in the **Walls** layer and select the three white lines by clicking on them.

5. This time you will move the lines to the **Walls** layer from their Properties window. Click on the small arrow next to the **Properties** tool group's title to open the panel with the same name.

6. The **Properties** panel opens as a floating panel on the left of the work area and displays the main characteristics of the three selected lines. Click on the **Layer** field in the panel's **General** section, open the list of layers, and choose the one called **Walls**.

7. Close the **Properties** panel by clicking on the X button in its **Title Bar** and, after noticing that all the lines are now in the **Walls** layer and display the color assigned to that layer, unselect the lines by pressing the **Escape** key.

8. Before finishing, let's see how to define the **Walls** layer as the current layer for the next objects you will draw in it. Go to the **Layer Property Manager** by clicking on the first icon in the **Layers** tool group.

9. Select the **Walls** layer in the Manager and click on the **Set current** icon, which looks like a green checkmark.

10. Close the **Layer Property Manager** and finish the exercise by saving your changes.

You can also go to an object's Properties panel by using the **Ctrl + 1** key shortcut.

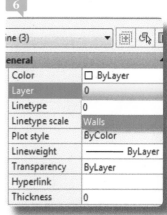

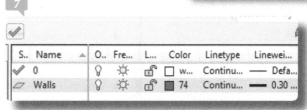

You can also define a layer as the current layer by selecting it in the manager and using the **Alt + C** key shortcut.

Locking and hiding layers

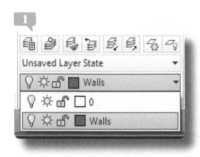
IN ORDER TO AVOID CHANGING objects in a layer by accident you can quickly and easily lock the layers they are in. You can also disable or hide layers to make all the objects they contain invisible in order to obtain a clearer vision of the complete drawing or to hide assistant objects as lines of reference.

1. In this exercise you will see how easy it is to lock and hide layers. You can carry out these actions both from the **Layer Property Manager** as well as from the **Layers** tool group, where layer properties are also displayed. By default, all layers are unlocked and visible, which implies that you can view and modify the items drawn in them. For starters, let's hide the **Walls** layer. Open the list of layers in the **Layers** tool group and click on the **Turn layer on or off** button, represented by a lightbulb. ▭

2. A dialog box asks you if you wish to turn the layer off, which will hide the objects it contains. Click on the **Turn Current Layer Off** option. ▭

3. As you can see, the square you drew in a previous exercise disappears from the work area. To turn the layer back on, simply click on the lightbulb icon –now displayed as unlit– in the **Walls** layer. However, you will now learn how to do this

When you turn a layer off, it will not be visible or available for printing, even if the **Draw** option is active.

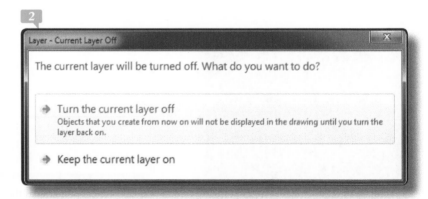

Turning layers off is done via the **Layer – Current Layer Off** dialog box.

from the Layer Properties Panel, which you will open from the Command Line. Type **layer** and press the **Return** key.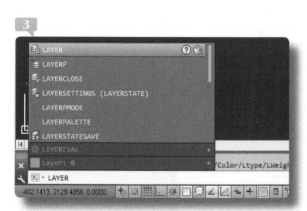

4. Notice that in the **On** column of the **Walls** layer an unlit light-bulb is also displayed, indicating that the layer is off. Click on this icon to turn the layer on again.

5. Let's lock the layer to prevent the drawings it contains from being altered. Click on the padlock icon for the **Walls** layer to lock it.

6. Close the **Layer Property Manager** by clicking on the X button in its **Title Bar**.

7. Now that the Walls layer is locked, you cannot manipulate the square. Click on any line in this object and select the **Move** tool in the **Modify** group.

8. Notice that the Command Line shows you that the object you selected is in a locked layer. Try selecting it again by clicking on it for this message to display again.

9. Indeed, locking layers prevents objects from being altered. To finish this exercise, unlock the Walls layer by clicking the padlock icon that appears in the **Layers** tool group.

020

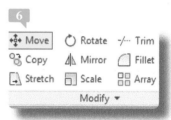

To select the Move tool, click **move + Return**.

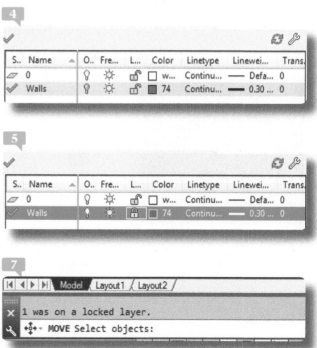

Keep in mind that the new **AutoComplete** function helps you to enter commands in the Command Line.

Other layer functions

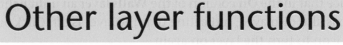

THE LAYER FUNCTIONS you learned about in the three previous exercises are the most basic and frequent ones you will encounter when working with layers. In this exercise you will see a few more that, in spite of being slightly less used, will be very useful to make your work with layers smoother and faster, which is essential when it comes to mastering AutoCAD.

1. Start with the **First drawing** file with which you have already worked in previous exercises.

2. Place the right and lower lines of your rectangle into **Layer 0**, as you learned in **exercise 19**.

3. In the Layers tool group, click on the second icon on the upper row, Set object layer as current, 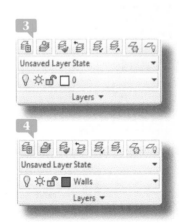 which takes you to the layer the selected object is in. Select a line from the rectangle in **Layer 0** and press the **Return** key. You will now be working in **Layer 0**.

4. Click on the fourth icon in the top line of the **Layers** tool group, Undo, that undoes your last change or series of changes to the Layer settings. Undoing the previous action takes you back to the **Walls** layer.

5. In the **Layers** tool group, click on the fifth icon on the upper row, **Isolate**, to hide or lock all layers except the one with the currently selected items. Select a white line in **Layer 0** and

press the Return button. The **Walls** layers is locked and the lines in it are grayed out. 5

6. In the **Layers** tool group, click on the sixth button on the top row, **Unisolate**, to restore all the layers that were hidden with the **Isolate** command. The **Walls** layer is unlocked and the lines it contains are once again displayed normally. 6

7. In the **Layers** tool group, open the **Layers** tab 7 and select the fifth icon on the lower line, **Change to current layer**, which changes the selected objects to the current layer. Select the lower white line in **Layer 0** and press the **Return** key. That line is moved to **Walls**, the current layer. 8

8. In the **Layers** tool group, open the **Layers** tab and click on the seventh icon in the lower line, **Layer Walk**, which looks like the objects in the selected layers and hides the other layers. Select the **Walls** layer and see how it only displays the lines included in that layer. The effect is temporary by default and the layers are restored once you close the dialog box. 9

9. New in AutoCAD 2014, the **Merge** function (you can access this function by selecting one or more layers in the **Layer Properties Manager** and then clicking with the right-hand mouse button) allows you to merge the selected layers into one new or one existing target layer and delete the previous ones. You cannot merge **Layer 0** or the current layer.

10. To finish this exercise, leave the four lines in the rectangle in the **Walls** layer.

Drawing lines

THE LINE TOOL DRAWS A LINE between two points, between geometric figures, or between two points chosen in any part of the graphic area or by typing the X and Y coordinates for each point or the distances and angles in the Command Line.

1. In this exercise you will learn how to use the **Line** drawing tool, by working on the **First drawing** file. Click on the **Line** tool in the **Draw** tool group.

2. Set the first point by typing the coordinates in that window or by clicking directly on the point of the graphic zone where you want the line to start. Type the coordinates **1000,850** in the Command Line to indicate where the line starts and press the **Return** key.

3. The **Polar tracking** function, the fifth icon in the **Status Bar**, is a visual aid that allows you to see the polar coordinates at the point indicated by the cursor. You can use this information to determine the second point or specify it with absolute coordinates. Type the coordinates **1000,2326** in the Command Line and press **Return**.

4. Notice how the Command Line still asks you for points for new lines. You will now use relative polar coordinates. Type the coordinates **@1430<0** in the Command Line and press the **Return** key.

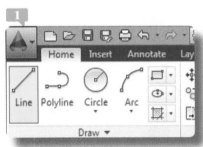

Line | Polyline | Circle | Arc

Draw ▼

You can activate the Line tool from the Command Line using the shortcut **I** + **Return**.

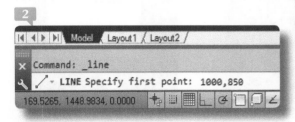

Command: _line

LINE Specify first point: 1000,850

169.5265, 1448.9834, 0.0000

5. The new line has now been drawn, without any angle, to the new specified point on the X-axis. To disable the **Line** tool, press the **Return** key.

6. Now let's say that, after disabling the Line tool, you would like to draw a new vertical line whose starting point is precisely the last point of the last line you drew. Click on the fourth button on the **Status Bar** to activate the **Ortho** command  and select the Line command again by clicking on the first icon in the **Draw** tool group.

7. To set the last point of the last line you drew as the first point, press the **Return** key.

8. To draw the new vertical line, type in the coordinates **2430,850** and press the **Return** key.

9. In order to close the rectangle you can use another drawing mode that will help you to easily locate the final point of the rectangle: the **Object Snap** mode, which is active by default in the Status Bar. Move the cursor to the lower part of the first line and, once you see a green indicator and the term **Endpoint**, click on it.

10. Press the **Return** key to leave the line drawing mode and click on the **Save** icon in the Quick Access Toolbar to finish this exercise.

IMPORTANT

The use of **Multifunctional Grips** that already existed for polylines and splines has been extended to lines and arcs. When locating the cursor on the ends of the selected lines, the **Stretch** grip, which allows you to stretch the line, appears.

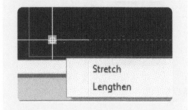

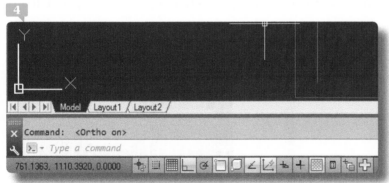

You can also enable the **Ortho** mode by pressing the F8 key.

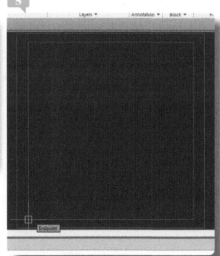

You can also save changes from the Application menu or by pressing the Ctrl + S shortcut.

Object Snap mode is the sixth icon in the Status Bar.

Creating rectangles

THERE ARE SPECIFIC TOOLS IN AUTOCAD that allow you to draw standard objects and shapes to save time. Such is the case of the Rectangle tool.

1. In this exercise you will use the **Rectangle** drawing tool to create several objects that will act as a table and a countertop for your floor plan. Let's begin by adding a layer to your drawing in which you will add furniture. Click on the **Layer properties** icon, the first in the **Layers** tool group.

2. In order to add a new layer, click on the **New layer** icon, the piece of paper and a yellow star, name it **Furniture**, and choose dark brown as its color.

3. With the new layer selected, click on the **Set current** button, the green checkmark sign, to indicate that objects will be drawn in this layer, and close the Layer Properties Manager by clicking on its X button.

4. To select the Rectangle tool, click on the first of the three icons in the vertical list in the **Drawing** tool group.

5. In order to create this geometric shape, you need to specify the coordinates for the points that represent its upper left and

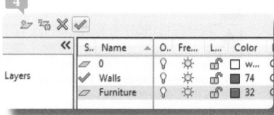

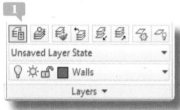

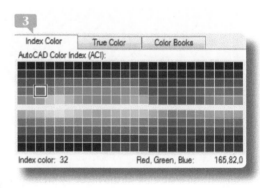

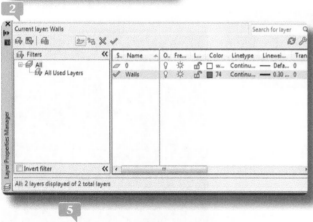

lower left vertices. Type the coordinates **12500,1000** in the Command Line and press the **Return** key.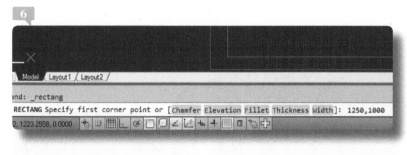

6. Once you have specified the rectangle's first vertex, AutoCAD will request the coordinates for the opposite vertex in order to define the height and width of the rectangle. Type the coordinates **1500,1500** and press **Return**.

7. Now that you have created the rectangle that simulates the table, let's create one that represents a countertop to which you will later add the stove. Click on the Command Line, type **rect** and choose the **Rectang** tool from the AutoComplete options list.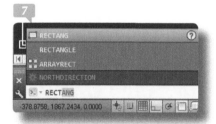

8. Click on the Command Line, type the coordinates **2105,2240** and press **Return** to place the first point of the new rectangle.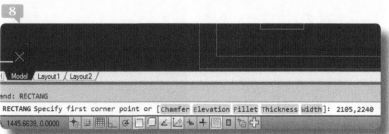

9. Type in the coordinates **2375,1995** and press the **Return** key.

10. You only need to draw one last rectangle, two of whose sides will meet with the walls. Select the Rectangle tool again by pressing the **Return** key.

11. Enter the coordinates **1000,2326** and press **Return**.

12. Type the coordinates **2000,2004**, press **Return**, 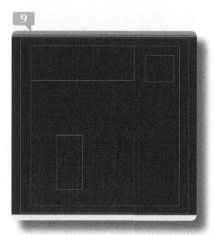 and save changes by clicking on the **Save** icon in the **Quick Access Toolbar**.

You can disable and configure the new **AutoComplete** function from the same option in the Command Line's pop-up menu.

Trimming and extending objects

THE TRIM AND EXTEND TOOLS allow you to shorten or lengthen certain objects to certain edges. Using the Trim tool, as with the similar Extend tool, involves two steps: the first is to select the reference lines, also called cutting edges, that determine the edge or edges with which you will cut a line down, and the second is to indicate which lines will be trimmed.

1. Draw a line by typing the coordinates **1700,1700** for the starting point and **2700,1700** for the final point.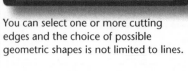

2. Click on the **Trim** tool in the **Modify** tool group.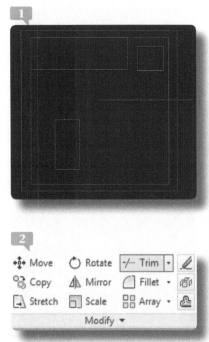

3. Choose the right side of the smaller rectangle in the **Walls** layer as a cutting edge.  Once you have selected the cutting edge, press the **Return** key to proceed with the trimming process.

4. Observe that, in the Command Line, the next step is to indicate which part of the object or which object you wish to trim. Click on the part of the line you drew earlier that is on the right of the cutting edge.

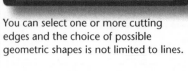

You can select one or more cutting edges and the choice of possible geometric shapes is not limited to lines.

5. Notice that the selected part of the line disappears from the drawing automatically.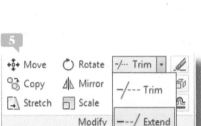

6. To finish the trimming process, press the **Return** key.

7. Click on the **Extend** pop-up tool in the **Modify** tool group.

8. Select the right side of the large rectangle in the Walls layer as the cutting edge. Once you have selected the limit, press the Return key to proceed with the extension process.

9. Notice that, in the Command Line, the next step is to indicate which part of the object or which object you wish to lengthen. Click on the right part of the line you drew first.

10. Notice that the selected part of the line extends automatically all the way to the specified limit.

11. As you know, you can press the Return key to finish the extension process and any other operation. Keep in mind that you can also do so by pressing the space bar or by selecting the Intro option in the pop-up menu that appears when right-clicking on the **graphic zone**. Perform this last action.

12. To finish this exercise, erase the line you have been working on.

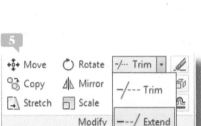

Commands with a small arrow next to them have drop-down menus that contain other commands.

You can select one or more cutting edges and the choice of possible geometric shapes is not limited to lines.

024

Working with the Offset tool

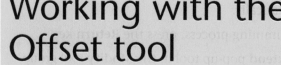

THE OFFSET TOOL ALLOWS YOU TO CREATE parallel entities, setting the distance between both or by pointing out which point they must cross.

1. In this exercise you will learn how to copy objects with the **Offset** command. To begin, click on the last icon in the **Modify** tool group, which corresponds to the **Offset** command.

2. As you can see in the Command Line, you can specify the distance between the two items or indicate a point that the new item should cross when working with this command. In this case you will keep the **Specify offset distance** that is active by default. Insert 20 and press the **Return** key.

3. Name the object you are going to move. Click on any part of the rectangle in the upper right corner of the floor plan.

4. You need to specify the point where the copy of this line will be created. Keep in mind that if you enable the **Multiple** option in the **Offset** tool you will be able to create several copies of the rectangle without having to use the tool again. Type in the coordinates **2150,2030** in the Command Line and press the **Return** key.

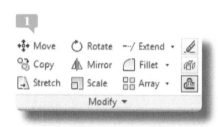

Keep in mind that not all objects can be modified with the **Offset** tool.

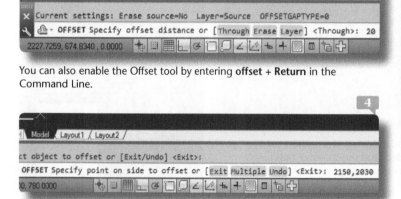

You can also enable the Offset tool by entering **offset** + **Return** in the Command Line.

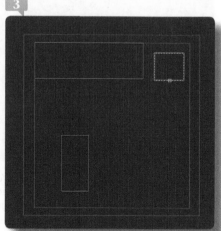

025

5. Notice that the **Offset** tool is still enabled and the Command Line still displays objects to be moved. Press the **Return** key to disable the **Offset** tool.

6. You will now round one of the corners using the **Chamfer** command; however, first, let's zoom on the zone that will be modified. Type **zoom** in the Command Line and press the **Return** key.

7. Type **w** and press **Return** To select **Window** zoom.

8. Drag a selection window that includes the offset rectangle and see how this zone becomes zoomed.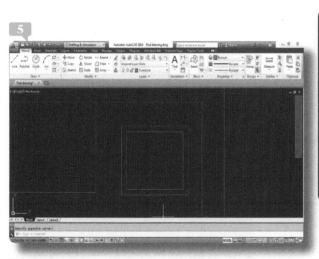

9. Type **chamfer** in the Command Line and press the **Return** key.

10. Before specifying the first line, let's change the distance the tool displays by default. Type **d** in the Command Line, press **Return**, enter 30 as the first chamfer distance and press **Return**.

11. Keep the value for the second distance in the chamfer by pressing the **Return** key, click on any point of the vertical line on the right of the inner rectangle to select it, and select the second line by clicking on any point on the upper horizontal line.

12. Notice how the corner where both lines intersect has become chamfered. Save changes with the **Ctrl + S** shortcut.

IMPORTANT

New in this AutoCAD version, you can use the **Chamfer** tool to close open polylines; this was not available in earlier versions.

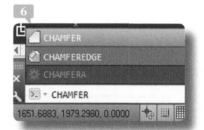

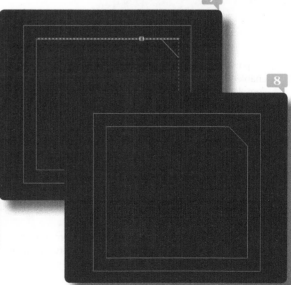

You can use the mouse directly on the work area to specify the **offset distance.**

Working with the Fillet tool

IMPORTANT

In the event that the radius of the curvature is superior to 0 and the fillet is applied to nonparallel lines, the effect obtained will be to round the vertex of their intersection. If, on the contrary, you use the **Fillet** tool on parallel lines, the resulting arc will be a perfect half-circle, and one of the lines will be lengthened or shortened automatically so that both ends are symmetrical.

THE FILLET MODIFICATION TOOL is used to round a vertex formed by two intersecting lines. AutoCAD allows you to set the curve radius so that if you give it the value 0, the lines will form an angular vertex, obtaining a perfect half-circle and now allowing you to "clean" the vertices formed by that lines.

1. In this exercise you will learn about two utilities in the **Fillet** modification tool. You will learn how to round vertices on the lower rectangle you edited earlier with the Chamfer tool. Type **fillet** in the Command Line and press **Return**.

2. You must now define the curvature's radius, which is 0 by default. Type the term ra in the Command Line, press Return, and, next to **Specify fillet radius**, enter 30 and press **Return** again.

3. You must now indicate which objects you want to modify. Click on the left side of the inner rectangle on the floor plan to select it, and then click on the upper side of that triangle. Notice how the upper left vortex becomes rounded.

4. To round the other corner, perform this operation again, using the **Fillet** tool each time.

5. Once you have modified these vertices, you will see how to

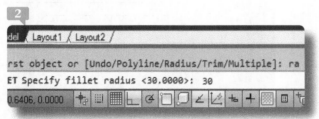

Keep in mind that you can also enable the tool by typing the complete command, **FILLET**, in the Command Line.

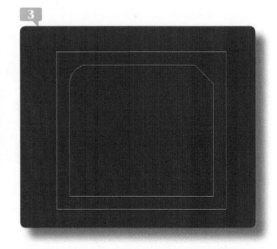

If you do not modify the value of the curvature, the lines you select will form an angular vertex. This is a very useful option if you want to delete vertices such as the ones formed by internal lines in a room.

026

use the **Fillet** tool to create an object representing a chair in this floor plan. To do this, draw two straight parallel lines and join them with a perfect semicircle. However, first, apply an **All** zoom to the drawing. Enter **zoom + Return** in the Command Line  type **A** and press **Return** again.

6. Click on the **Line** command in the **Draw** tool group.

7. In order to draw a line you must specify the coordinates for its starting and final points. Type the coordinates **1500,1320** in the Command Line, press **Return**, type the coordinates **1650,1320** and press **Return** twice.

8. Turn the Line tool on again by pressing the Return key, type the coordinates **1500,1200** for the first point in the second line, press **Return** and enter the coordinates **1650,1200** for the second point and press **Return** twice.

9. Once you have drawn the two lines, you can join them with an arc by using the **Fillet** tool. Click on **Fillet**, the second icon in the vertical list in the **Modify** tool group.

10. Click on the rightmost point of the upper line you just drew to select it, click on the right point of the lower line and notice that both are joined by a half-circle.

11. To finish, save your changes by pressing the **Save** icon in the **Quick Access Toolbar.**

IMPORTANT

New to this AutoCAD 2014 version is the ability to apply the **Fillet** tool to close open polylines; this was not available in earlier versions.

When joining two parallel lines there is no need to specify the curvature's radius as the result will always be a perfect half-circle connecting both ends, lengthening or shortening them if necessary.

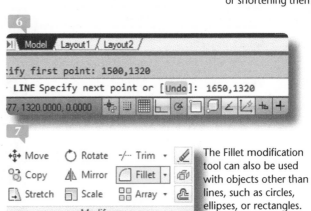

The Fillet modification tool can also be used with objects other than lines, such as circles, ellipses, or rectangles.

Rotating objects

ALL ITEMS IN AN AUTOCAD DRAWING can be modified in terms of both size and position. You can use the Rotate tool to turn items.

1. In this exercise you will learn how to use the Rotate tool by practicing changing the direction of the item that represents a stove in the upper right corner of your sample drawing, **First drawing**. To begin, click on the **Rotate** command in the **Modify** tool group.

2. As you can see by the Command Line, you need to select the elements you are going to rotate. Click on the two brown rectangles in the upper left corner of the floor plan and press **Return** to indicate that you are done selecting items.

3. The next step is to indicate which base point or axis upon which the object will be rotated. Type the coordinates **2240,1995** in the Command Line and press the **Return** key to confirm it.

4. Once you have set the rotation axis, AutoCAD requests the value of the rotation angle in degrees. Enter **-45** in the Command Line and press **Return**.

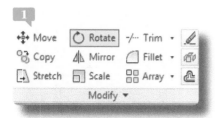

To activate the Rotate tool from the Command Line, type **rot** or **rotate** and press the **Return** key.

You can set the **base point** by clicking directly on the graphic zone or by inputting its coordinates in the Command Line, the latter method being far more accurate.

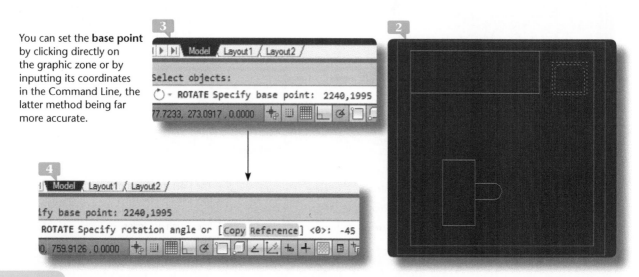

027

5. Notice how the position of the rectangles has changed. Let's rotate the object that represents the chair counterclockwise. Enter **rot** in the Command Line and press the **Return** key.

6. Click on the two lines and the arc you obtained after using the **Fillet** tool and press the **Return** key to confirm your selection.

7. Specify the base point. Type the coordi-nates **1370,1265** in the Command Line and press **Return**.

8. For the chair to rotate toward the left, that is, counterclockwi-se, type the positive value **90** in the Command Line and press the **Return** key.

9. You have now rotated the stove and the chair in contrary directions. As you can see, you have easily mastered the use of the **Rotate** tool and can now finish this exercise. Save your changes by clicking on the **Save** icon in the **Quick Access Toolbar**.

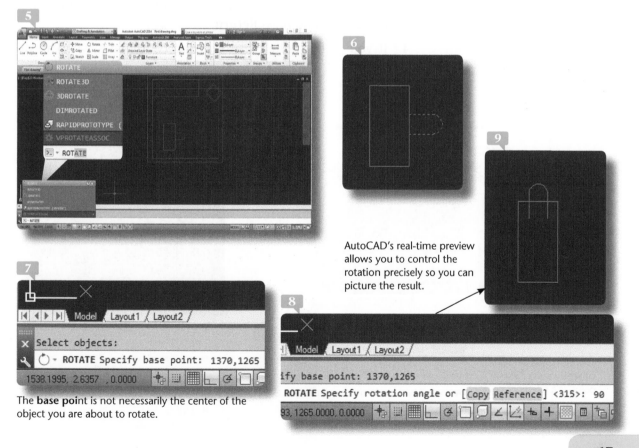

AutoCAD's real-time preview allows you to control the rotation precisely so you can picture the result.

The **base point** is not necessarily the center of the object you are about to rotate.

Moving objects

THE MOVE TOOL allows you to move selected objects across a certain distance and in a certain direction. You can activate this tool from the Modify tool group as well as from the Command Line, using **move + Return**.

1. In this exercise you will learn how to move objects in Auto-CAD. Your goal is to change the location of the rectangles that simulate the stove you rotated in the previous exercise. Click on the **Move** command in the **Modify** tool group.

2. Click on the two brown rectangles on the upper right corner and press the **Return** key.

3. Set a base point where the move will start. If you enable the **Move** function, it will use the coordinates 0,0 as the base point. In this case, you will use the approximate center of the object as the base point. To do this, type the coordinates **2322,2082** and press **Return**.

4. If you prefer, rather than entering coordinates, you can di-

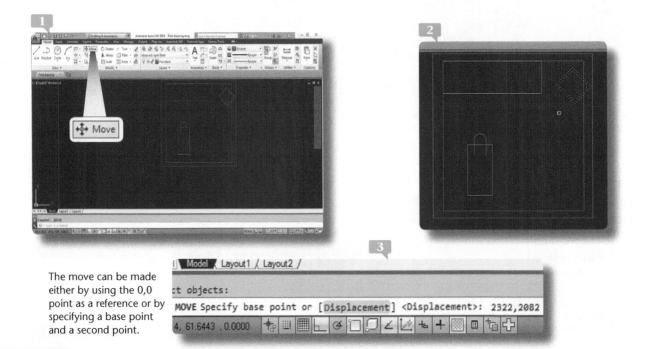

The move can be made either by using the 0,0 point as a reference or by specifying a base point and a second point.

028

rectly click on the object's center. You must specify the second reference point in the move. As you know, you can do so graphically, by clicking on the point where you want the object to move, or by inputting coordinates. Before doing so, select the **Ortho** mode by pressing the **F8** key or clicking on the **Ortho** icon.

5. As you already saw in a previous exercise, the **Ortho** mode allows you to restrict cursor movements to horizontal and vertical moves in order to achieve a higher degree of precision when creating and modifying objects. Type the coordinates **2246,1952** in the Command Line and press **Enter**.

6. Notice how the object moves to the specified point. Keep in mind that you can also move an object a relative distance by specifying the coordinate value for the first point and pressing **Return** for the second. In this case, the coordinates are used as a relative move rather than a base point. To finish this exercise, click on the **Save** icon in the **Quick Access Toolbar**.

IMPORTANT

Most experienced AutoCAD users know the number of most commands by memory, but newer users probably won't. In order to speed up your use of the Command Line, simply start writing a system variable or command and the new **AutoComplete** feature will display the different options; it will therefore be very easy for you to find the appropriate commands. Likewise, the **Recent Commands** feature in the Command Line's pop-up menu allows you to use the last values and commands you used without having to type them in again.

To select **Ortho** mode you can also use the fourth icon on the **Status Bar**.

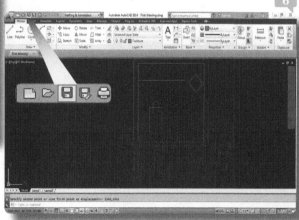

You can also move an object a relative distance by specifying the coordinate value for the first point and pressing **Return** for the second. In this case, the coordinates are used as a relative move rather than as a base point.

Aligning objects

THE ALIGN COMMAND, included among the operations in the Modify tool group, allows you to align objects with one another by moving and rotating them. The aligning process is based on a series of source and destination points, specified for each object. When activating any of these commands and after selecting the objects you wish to align, AutoCAD will ask you to specify one or two pairs of source and destination points.

1. In this exercise you will learn how to align objects. To begin, draw a line in your **First drawing** file, which you will later align with one of the existing objects. Click on the **Line** tool icon in the **Draw** group and type **1900,1000** as the start coordinates and **1900,1800** as the end coordinates, then press **Return** to quit the tool.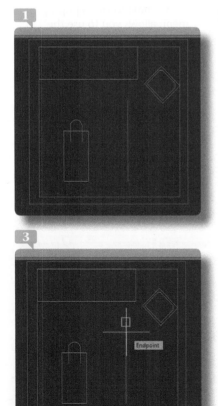

2. Select the new line by clicking on it and enable the Align tool, the first icon in the second row in the drop-down menu in the **Modify** group.

3. You can also activate this tool by typing **align + Return** in the Command Line. Click on the upper end of the line to set it as the first source point for alignment. With **Object Snap**

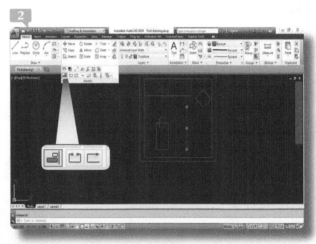

In order to access commands that are not visible at first sight, simply click on the arrow button that opens a drop-down menu, in this case, in the **Modify** tab.

029

enabled, with the cursor on the line, you should wait for **Endpoint** to appear to select it.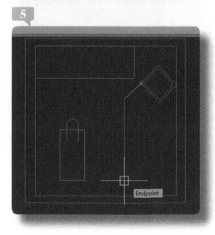

4. For the **first destination point** (where the **first source point** will be moved), choose the upper left vertex of the large rectangle you rotated earlier.

5. Click on the lower end of the line to set it as the **second source point**.

6. Choose the lower left vertex of the rectangle you rotated earlier as the **second destination point**.

7. When prompted for the third point, press **Return** as the third point is only used to align 3D objects. Press **Return** again to indicate that you do not want to scale the line in this case.

8. Notice that your line is automatically placed on the side of the rectangle you specified.

9. To finish this exercise, save your changes by clicking on the Save icon in the Quick Access Toolbar.

IMPORTANT

You will use these steps a lot when working with AutoCAD, so it is crucial that you become familiar with doing this. You only need three points when aligning 3D objects.

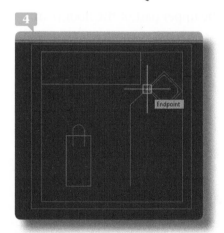

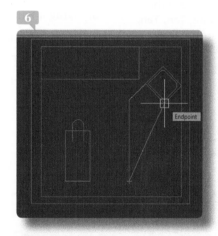

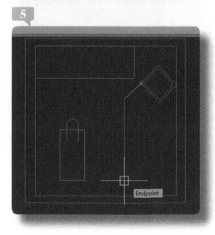

Keep in mind that you need to wait for **Endpoint** to appear before selecting it in order to ensure that you have selected the correct end.

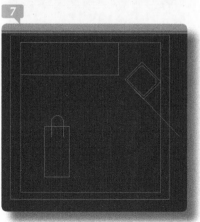

Drawing circles

CIRCLES ARE ONE OF THE MOST USED basic shapes in AutoCAD. They are often used to represent holes, wheels, hoops, arches, columns, trees, etc. You can either enable the Circle tool by selecting it in the Drawing tool group or by typing the appropriate command, **c + Return** in the Command Line.

1. In this exercise you will learn how to use the **Circle** tool to draw these shapes that will be used to represent the burners on the stove as well as a sink in the **First drawing** floor plan. Apply a Window zoom to the part of the floor plan you are going to be working with. Enter **zoom** in the Command Line and press the **Return** key.

2. Type **w** and press Return again To select **Window** zoom mode.

3. Drag a window that covers the upper part of the floor plan.

4. Click on the Circle icon in the Drawing tool group to draw in the **Center, Radius** mode.

5. Place the center of the first circle on top of the two rectangles.

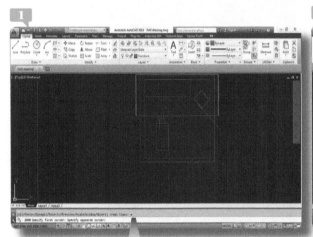

```
Center/Dynamic/Extents/Previous/Scale/Window/Object] ‹
ZOOM Specify first corner: Specify opposite corner:
```

The Circle option in the Drawing tool group contains a sub-menu that allows you to choose one of six different creation modes.

Type the coordinates **2240,2045** in the Command Line and press the **Return** key.

6. Specify the length of the circle's radius. Enter **30** in the Command Line and press the **Return** key.

7. You have now created your first circle. Repeat these steps to create a bigger circle that will act as the sink, this time using the **Circle Center Diameter** tool. Click on the arrow button of the **Circle** tool and choose the appropriate option.

8. Type in the coordinates **1614,2130** and press the **Return** key to set them as the center point.

9. You must now specify the circle's diameter. Enter **180** in the Command Line and press the **Return** key to create the circle.

10. As you can see, drawing circles is easy. Based on the mode you have chosen for the Circle tool you will need to specify certain values, as prompted in the Command Line. In the next exercises you will use these circles to see how the **Copy and Create Symmetries** tools work. To finish, save your changes by using the **Ctrl + S** shortcut.

You can disable tooltips from the **Viewing** tab in the Program Options window.

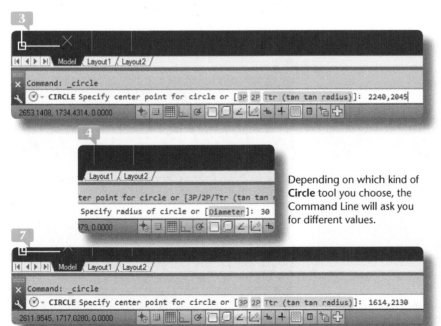

Depending on which kind of **Circle** tool you choose, the Command Line will ask you for different values.

Copying objects

IMPORTANT

In order to use the Copy tool more precisely, you can use coordinates and other visual aids such as **Grid Snap** or **Object Snap**.

THE COPY MODIFICATION TOOL, which is also included in the Modify tool group, allows you to obtain exact copies of selected objects. Once it is active, you need to set two points, a base point, which acts as the reference point where the copying begins, and a second point that acts as the final point for the copy. This defines a vector that indicates the distance and direction in which the copied objects must move.

1. In this exercise you will learn how to use the **Copy** tool to obtain an exact duplicate of the circles you drew in the previous exercise in your **First drawing** example file. Click on the **Copy** command in the **Modify** tool group.

2. Click on the border of the larger circle and press **Return** to exit Select mode.

3. You must now set a base point by clicking on the work area or by typing the corresponding coordinates in the Command Line. Remember that the distance by which the copied object will be displaced is equivalent to the distance between the base point and the displacement point. In this case, click on the center of the circle to select it as the base point.

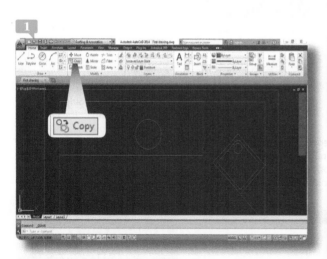

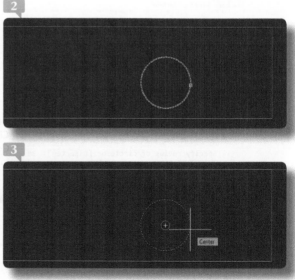

You can also activate the Copy tool from the Command Line by entering **copy** + **Return** or **cp** + **Return**.

031

4. The base point must not necessarily be a point located in the object you are going to copy: You can choose any point in the work area, as the move is defined by the relative position between this point and the displacement point. Next, move the cursor to the left, in a straight line, and click when the copy of the circle is approximately one centimeter away from the original.

5. Move the cursor and notice that the Copy tool is still active, which means that you can make as many copies of the selected object as you like in this mode. Now, disable the **Copy** tool by pressing the **Return** key again and activate it again by pressing **Return** one more time.

6. Select the small circle and press the **Return** key.

7. Click on the center of the object to set it as the base point. Drag the cursor diagonally downward and click when the copy of the circle is approximately a centimeter and a half away from the original.

8. Press **Return** again to leave the Copy tool and to see the final result. Finish the exercise by clicking on the **Save** icon in the **Quick Access Toolbar**.

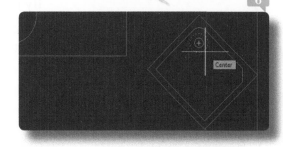

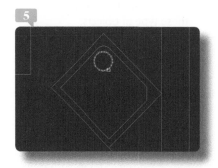

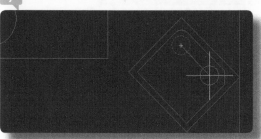

You can specify the distance from the original object where you want the copy to be placed by dragging the cursor or entering the coordinates in the Command Line.

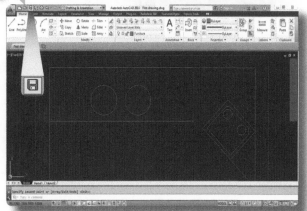

Erasing objects

ONE OF THE MOST USED ACTIONS IN AUTOCAD is erasing objects, and the program includes several ways of doing this. The Erase tool, in the Quick Access Toolbar, can be used to delete any item in a drawing. You can also select the object and press the Delete key or use the appropriate option in its pop-up menu to do this.

1. In this exercise you will learn how to erase objects in different ways, and you will erase several lines from your **First drawing** example. Apply a Window zoom on the sloped line you aligned previously. Insert **Zoom** in the Command Line and press the **Return** key.

2. Type **w** in the Command Line, press the Return key, and drag a zoom window over the zone in which the objects you are going to erase are located.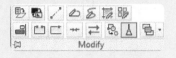

3. Make a copy of this line.

4. Click on the **Erase** icon, shown as a pencil eraser, in the **Modify** tool group.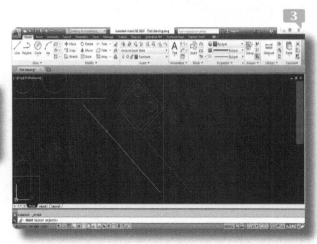

5. Select the item or items to be erased. Click on the line on the left to select it.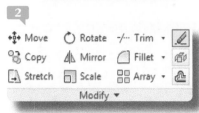

The Erase tool can also be activated by entering erase + Return in the Command Line.

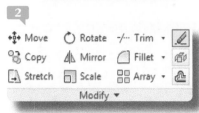

When selecting the **Erase** tool, the command that appears in the Command Line is **_erase**.

032

6. You can keep on selecting objects in the graphic zone, but, in this case, since you are going to learn more methods for erasing, only choose this line. Press Return and notice that it has been erased.

7. Apart from the **Erase** tool, you can use the **Delete** key to delete objects in a drawing from your keyboard. Click on the original line to select it 🔲 and press the **Delete** key to make it disappear.

8. Here's another method to delete objects. Undo the last operation by clicking on the **Undo** icon in the **Quick Access Toolbar**. 🔲

9. Select the original line again and right-click on it to open its pop-up menu.

10. You can see that many of the object editing tools are also located in this pop-up menu. Choose the **Erase** option. 🔲

11. To apply an **Extents** zoom to the drawing and see it in its entirety, click on the third icon in the **Navigation Bar**, which is displayed to the right of the work area. 🔲

12. Save your changes by clicking on the **Save** icon in the **Quick Access Toolbar.**

The **Zoom Extents** viewing tool displays all the objects in a drawing.

If you make a mistake when deleting an object, you can use the Undo tool to recover it.

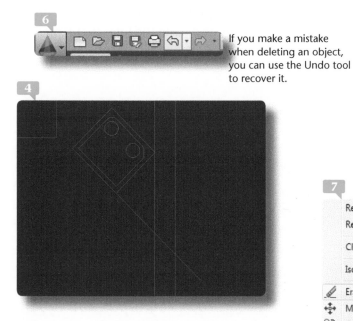

You can select the object first and enable the **Erase** tool later; the results are the same.

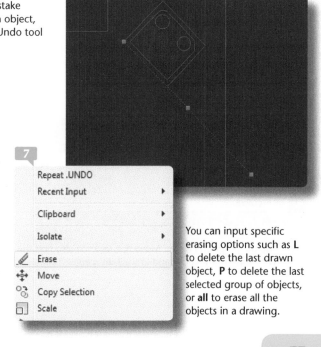

7
Repeat .UNDO
Recent Input ▶
Clipboard ▶
Isolate ▶
✐ Erase
✛ Move
⊙ Copy Selection
▱ Scale

You can input specific erasing options such as **L** to delete the last drawn object, **P** to delete the last selected group of objects, or **all** to erase all the objects in a drawing.

Copying with a base point

THE BASE POINT IS THE INITIAL REFERENCE POINT for the most commonly used modification commands, Copy, Move, Rotate, Stretch, and Scale, and it is also the insertion point for a drawing. The **Copy with Base Point** option is complemented by the **Paste to Original Coordinates** command.

1. In this exercise you will learn how to copy some objects from your current floor plan, **First drawing**, to a new document by using the **Copy with Base Point** command, with which you can copy objects with a specified base point. You can enable this command from the object's pop-up menu, entering **copybase + Return** in the Command Line or by using the **Ctrl + Shift + C** shortcut. To begin, enter **copybase** in the Command Line and press the **Return** key.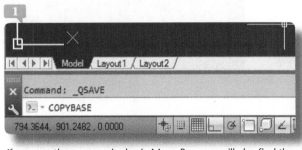

2. You must specify which point in the drawing will be used as the coordinate to paste the objects from the current drawing that you will copy to the Clipboard. Type the coordinates **1375,1255** in the Clipboard and press the **Return** key.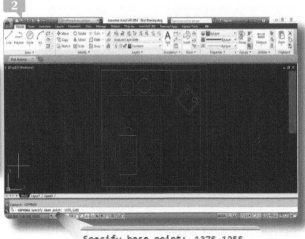

3. Place all the objects you are going to paste in the new document. In this case, let's copy and paste the lines that represent

If you use the program's classic Menu Bar, you will also find the **Copy with base point** command in the **Edit** menu.

Specify base point: 1375,1255

033

the walls. Click on each one of the lines that represent these items on the Green floor plan and, once you're done selecting, press **Return**.

4. Click on the **New** icon in the **Quick Access Toolbar** and open a new document based on the **acadiso.dwt** template.

5. Paste the elements you just copied. Click on the arrow below the **Paste** command in the **Clipboard** tool group and choose the **Paste to Original Coordinates** option.

6. To check that all the copied lines have been pasted correctly, apply an Extents zoom to the drawing. Click on the third icon in the Navigation Bar.

7. All the items you copied to the Clipboard have been pasted on the same coordinates as in the original drawing. To finish this exercise, close the new document without saving your changes. Click on the X button in its work area.

8. Confirm that you do not want to save changes by pressing the **No** button in the dialog box to return to the **First drawing** file.

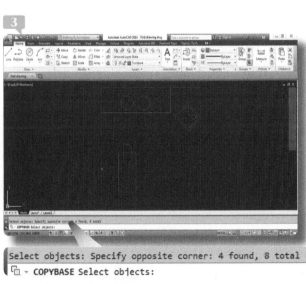

Select objects: Specify opposite corner: 4 found, 8 total
COPYBASE Select objects:

The **number of selected items** is indicated in the Command Line.

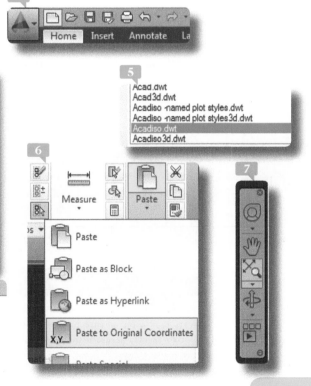

Creating arrays with the Copy tool

THE COPY TOOL includes the Array feature, which allows you to create a specific amount of objects distributed at a specific distance. The Array function after entering the base point for the Copy command.

IMPORTANT

The **Adjust** parameter in the Copy tool's Array function places the final copy of the array in the specified displacement and makes the others adjust along a linear matrix between the original selection and the final copy.

`▾ COPY Specify second point or [Fit]:`

1. In this exercise you will learn about the **Array** feature in the Copy command, which you will use to generate several copies of an object with a specific distance between them. For example, let's practice with the large circle on the right. Select the **Copy** tool in the **Modify** tool group.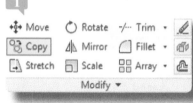

2. Select the large circle on the right and press the **Return** key to confirm your selection. 🔳

3. You need to set the base point from which the move will take place. In this case, click on the approximate center of the selected object. 🔳

4. Remember that if you enable the **Object Snap** function in the Status Bar, AutoCAD will display specific points for objects, such as the center point. Once you have set the first base point, you can either specify a second point or enable the **Array** function. Type m in the Command Line and press the **Return** key. 🔳

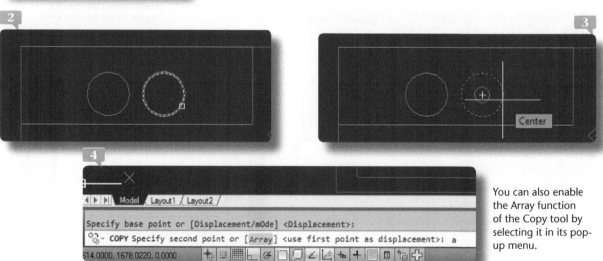

You can also enable the Array function of the Copy tool by selecting it in its pop-up menu.

5. You need to specify the number of items in the array, including the entire original selection. Enter 5 in the Command Line and press the **Return** key. 5

6. The Command Line now requests a second point. This point determines a direction and a distance for the array relative to the base point. By default, the first copy of the array is placed in the specified displacement and the rest is spread along a linear array beyond that point with the same incremental displacement. You can see the resulting effect depending on the applied distance by moving the mouse. Click approximately one centimeter away diagonally to the right and see how the array is generated. 6

7. The **Copy** tool is still active, so you could still create more copies or arrays. 7 Disable the **Copy** tool by pressing the **Return** key.

8. As you will see later on in exercises on rectangular and polar arrays, the objects that make them up behave independently. Once you have seen how the Copy tool's **Array** mode works, finish this exercise by erasing all the circles created by the array. Select the four last circles 8 and click on the **Erase** icon in the **Modify** tool group. 9

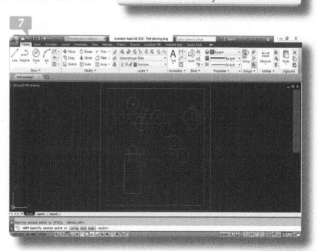

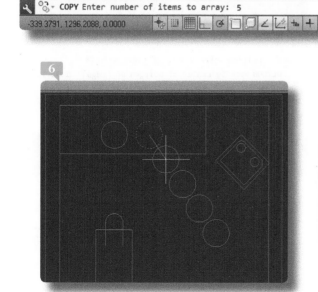

Drawing polygons

IMPORTANT

AutoCAD allows you to draw polygons with a minimum of 3 sides and a maximum of 1,024. To do this, you need to input some basic information: the number of sides, the exact location of the polygon's center point, and its radius to set its size. You must also specify whether it would be inscribed or circumscribed to the circle.

AUTOCAD ALLOWS YOU TO QUICKLY DRAW REGULAR POLYGONS that is, equiangular and equilateral polygons, with the Polygon drawing tool.

1. In this exercise you will learn how to create inscribed and circumscribed polygons in AutoCAD. To begin, click on the arrow button of the Rectangle drawing tool and choose the **Polygon** tool.

2. As you can see in the Command Line, the program first prompts you to enter the number of sides. Enter 10 and press the **Return** key.

3. Next, set the coordinates for the center point of the polygon. Type the coordinates **1375,1155** in the Command Line and press the **Return** key to confirm the input.

4. Indicate whether the polygon will be inscribed or circumscribed to the circle that defines it. Type **i** in the Command Line and press **Return**.

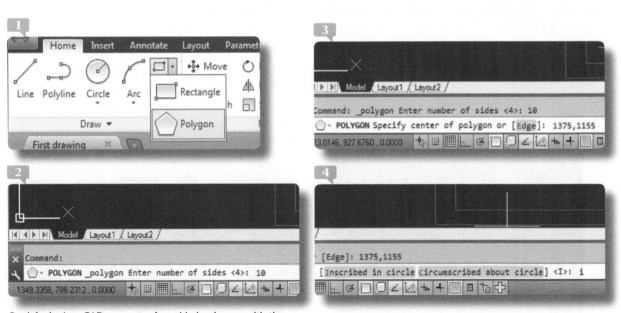

By default, AutoCAD generates four-sided polygons with the **Polygon** tool.

035

5. The polygon is inscribed in its circle, that is, all its vertices fall on the circumference that surrounds it. You only need to set the polygon's radius. Enter 75 in the Command Line and press the **Return** key.

6. You have now drawn your first polygon. Carry out the same steps again to create a five-sided circumscribed polygon with the same center as the one you just created. In order to re-enable the **Polygon** tool, press **Return**.

7. Enter **5** in the Command Line and press the **Return** key.

8. For the center of the shape to be the same as the one in the last shape you drew, you can use the @ symbol. Type in this symbol and press **Return**.

9. In order to make the new polygon be circumscribed to its circumference, type **c** and press **Return**.

10. You must specify the polygon's radius, which in this case should be the same as the one for the previous polygon, so that, being a circumscribed polygon, it will be larger than the inscribed one. Type 75 in the Command Line and press the **Return** key.

11. See the results. To finish this exercise, save the changes made to the drawing by clicking on the **Save** icon in the **Quick Access Toolbar**.

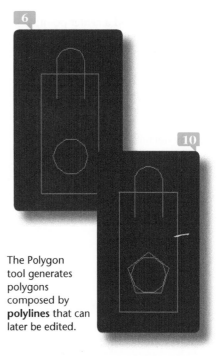

The Polygon tool generates polygons composed by **polylines** that can later be edited.

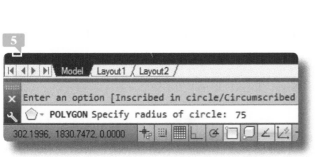

You can set the radius of a polygon graphically by clicking on the graphic zone or by typing the exact value in the Command Line

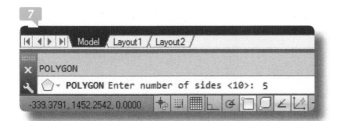

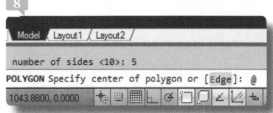

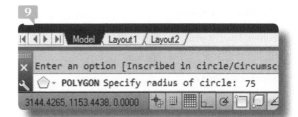

Drawing arcs

THE ARC DRAWING TOOL is mainly used to represent a door or window swing in floor plans. Generally, both items are usually shown open at a 90-degree angle to see the space they take up and in which direction they open.

1. In this exercise you will learn how to create an arc that will be used to represent a door swing in your floor plan. To begin, add a new layer to your drawing. Go to the **Layer Properties Manager** by clicking on the first icon in the **Layers** tool group, click on the **New layer** icon in this panel, type in **Doors and windows** 1 and press **Return**.

2. To define this new layer as the current layer, click on the icon that looks like a green checkmark.

3. Click on this layer's color sample, choose **Yellow** 2 and, after applying it, close the **Manager**.

4. Let's create a door by using a straight line and an arc. To begin, specify the point where it will be located on the lower wall. Open the **Modify** tool group and click on the second command in the second row, which is the **Split** command. 3

5. This tool is used to split a line in two; you will learn more about it later on. You now need to specify the initial and

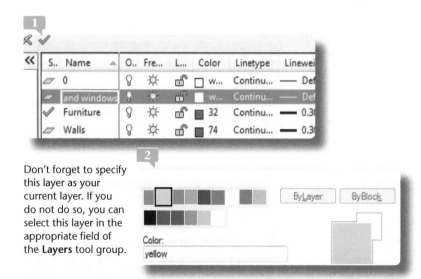

Don't forget to specify this layer as your current layer. If you do not do so, you can select this layer in the appropriate field of the **Layers** tool group.

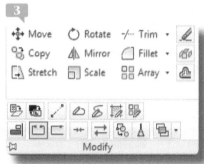

You can also enable the Split tool using the **split** + **Return** in the Command Line

final points of the split. Type the coordinates **2240,851** in the Command Line and press **Return**.

6. Now, as the second point for the break, type in the coordinates **1980,851** and press **Return** again.

7. Notice how the lower line has automatically been split in two. The space between the two lines will act as the door. Next, draw a vertical line as long as the blank space you just created. Type l in the Command Line and press **Return** To select the **Line** command.

8. Set the starting point in the opening as the starting point for the door. Type in the coordinates **2240,851** and press **Return**.

9. Type in the coordinates **2240,1095** to locate the end of the line at this point and press **Return** two times in a row.

10. Draw the arc that will represent the surface covered by the door when opening. In the **Drawing** tool group, click on the **3-Point** creation mode in the **Arc** command icon.

11. Type in the coordinates **1980,850** and press **Return** to set this point as the starting point for the arc, enter **2240,1095** as the center point and press **Return**.

12. Finally, type in the coordinates **2241,1095** and press **Return** to finish creating the arc and finish the exercise by saving your changes using the **Ctrl + S** shortcut.

036

IMPORTANT

Como novedad en esta versión de AutoCAD, tenemos la posibilidad de invertir la dirección de un arco presionando la tecla **Ctrl** a medida que lo dibujamos.

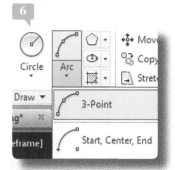

You can enable this tool from the **Drawing** tool group or by entering **arc** + **Return** in the Command Line.

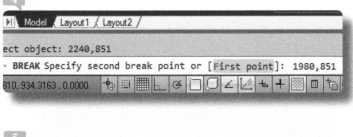

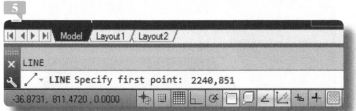

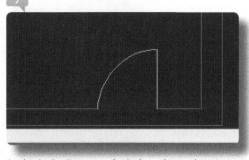

As this is the **Doors and windows** layer, the objects you draw in it are **yellow**, as you specified when creating the layer.

Drawing polylines

A POLYLINE IS A SPECIAL KIND OF LINE that treats several segments as a single entity; it can include arcs, it can be softened into a curve, and it can include several widths.

1. In this exercise you will use the **Polyline** tool to add an object that will represent the sink in your floor plan. You can find a copy of the example file, called **First drawing 2.dwg**, in the download section on our website. Go to the **Furniture** layer from the drop-down menu in the **Layers** tool group.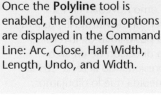

2. To select the **Polyline** tool, type pol in the Command Line and select the first option that appears in the **AutoComplete** menu.

3. Type the coordinates **1377,2245** in the Command Line and press **Return** to place the first point in the polyline.

4. Before setting the next point, increase the width of the line. Type **w**, pres **Return**, enter **1**, press **Return**, and enter **1** again and press **Return** for the initial and final width to be the same.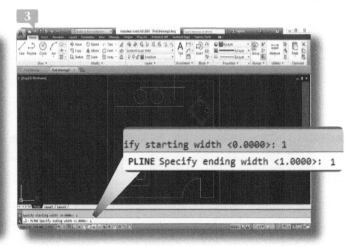

5. Once you have set the width of the polyline, continue creating the object by specifying the following points. Type the coordinates **1613,2245** and press **Return**.

If you prefer, you can enable the **Polyline** command by clicking on the appropriate icon in the **Drawing** tool group.

037

6. To define the first arc in the polyline, type **a** and press the **Return** key.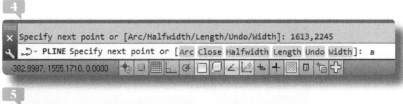

7. Place the final point of the arc at the coordinates **1613,2017** and press the **Return** key.

8. Enable the **Line** function of the **Polyline** tool by typing **n** and pressing **Return**.

9. Enter the coordinates **1377,2017** and press Return to define the next point in the line.

10. Type **a + Return** in the Command Line again To select the **Arc** mode of the **Polyline** tool.

11. To finish the polyline, type **cl** in the Command Line and press the **Return** key.

12. You have now created a new shape whose components behave like a single object. Select the polyline by clicking on it and right-click to open its pop-up menu.

13. Click on the **Polyline** option and select **Edit Polyline**.

14. To increase this polyline's width, type **w** and press the **Return** key.

15. Type **2** as the new width for all the segments in the polyline and press **Return** to see the results.

16. Press **Return** to finish editing the polyline and save your changes on the drawing by clicking on the **Save** icon in the **Quick Access Toolbar**.

IMPORTANT

When you need to make the final point meet the starting point, you should enable the **Object Snap** drawing mode to make them meet exactly. You can do it from the Status Bar or by pressing the F3 key.

4

Specify next point or [Arc/Halfwidth/Length/Undo/Width]: 1613,2245

PLINE Specify next point or [Arc Close Halfwidth Length Undo Width]: a

-382.9987, 1555.1710, 0.0000

5

Specify endpoint of arc or

PLINE [Angle CEnter CLose Direction Halfwidth Line Radius Second pt Undo Width]: 1

3257.7499, 970.7178 , 0.0000

In order To select any of the options related to the currently active tool, you need to enter the **capital** letter that appears in the action you wish to carry out.

Using the Spline command

IMPORTANT

Several improvements have been added to the Spline feature since AutoCAD 2011. Whereas, in AutoCAD 2011, **multifunctional grips** allowed you to add, stretch, specify, and change the direction of lines' tangents, you can also add and relocate vertices and turn segments into arcs since the last version. There is even an option that assists you to make the spline go where you want it to.

A SPLINE IS A SOFT CURVE CREATED by specifying through which points it must pass and by controlling how closely the curve must follow those points. This closeness is measured in degrees and is called tolerance. The Spline command is included in the Drawing tool group, and it can also be enabled from the Command Line by entering **spline + Return**.

1. In this exercise you will create a new object with the **Spline** drawing tool. Click on the arrow in the **Drawing** tool group and select the first icon in the drop-down menu, **Spline fit**.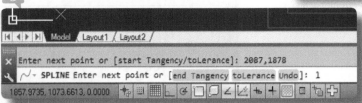

2. You will now draw a closed NURBS curve to simulate an irregular-shaped carpet. The first step is to specify where the first point in the spline will be located. Type the coordinates **2015,1850** in the Command Line and press the **Return** key.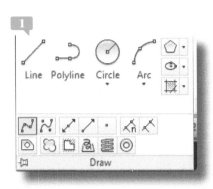

3. Specify which points will define the spline's path. Type the coordinates **2087,1878** and press **Return**.

4. Before setting more control points, adjust the tolerance level. Remember that tolerance is used to measure how closely

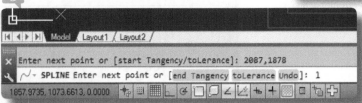

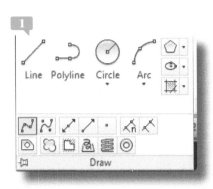

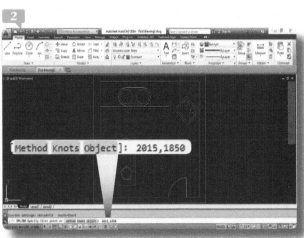

Splines, apart from being composed by Bezier arcs, can also be defined with fit points, as in this example, as well as control vertices located outside the line.

the spline will follow the fit points. To change it, type **l** and press **Return**.

5. As you can see, the default tolerance is 0 degrees. Enter **12** and press **Return**.

6. Now that you have set the tolerance, indicate more points and, finally, close the shape. Type the coordinates **2208,1764** and press **Return**.

7. Insert the coordinates **2083,1735** and press **Return**.

8. Type in the coordinates **2005,1753** and press **Return**.

9. You can finish the drawing so that the shape is open by pressing the **Return** key twice, or you can close it by using the appropriate function in the **Spline** tool. In this case, type c in the Command Line and press **Return** to close the shape.

10. Before finishing, You can turn a polyline into a spline by using the **Spline** function in the **Edit Polyline** command, even though the results will never be as precise as those you get with the **Spline** tool. Finish this exercise by saving your changes, using the **Ctrl + S** shortcut.

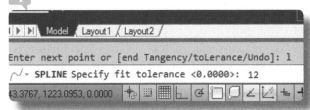

The **Tolerance** value specifies the distance to which the spline may deviate from the fit points. The default tolerance value, 0, means that the resulting spline must directly pass through all the fit points. The tolerance value is applied to all fit points except for the starting and ending points, which always have 0 tolerance.

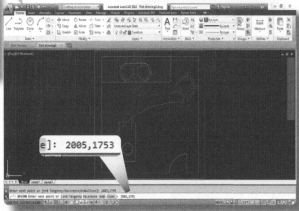

The process of creating a spline is very simple and involves specifying the fit points that will define the curve and adjusting tolerance. In order to close the curve so that the last point coincides with the first one and so that the curve is tangent to the union, you must use the **Close** option.

The Spline drawing allows you to draw **NURBS** (Non-Uniform Rational B-Spline) curves, which generate soft curves between the specified fit points.

Drawing freehand sketches

IMPORTANT

For any type of sketch, you must establish the minimum length (dimension) of the **line segments**. Short line segments may be more accurate, but they increase the size of the file considerably.

IF YOU NEED TO CREATE IRREGULAR OUTLINES or carry out tracking tasks with a digitizer, the Sketching tool is very useful since it allows you to draw sketches freehand. Such sketches are made up of several line segments that form a line, a polyline, or a spline. In the case of splines, you can establish the accuracy with which the spline will adapt to the freehand sketch.

1. During this exercise you will learn how to produce a freehand sketch. Before you start, check that the **CELTYPE** system variable is set on the **BYLAYER** line type. Click on the Command Line, type **CEL** and select the **Celtype** option from the **Auto-Complete** feature.

2. The default line type is **BYLAYER**, therefore objects will be created with the type of line assigned to the present layer, Furniture. Click on the **enter** key to confirm the default.

3. In order to activate the **Sketch** tool, type sketch in the Command Line and click on the **enter** key.

4. The parameters that can be defined for the Sketch tool and that are already visible on the Command Line are the type of object (line, polyline, or spline), the increment and the tolerance. As you can see, AutoCAD uses the **Line** type of object to create sketches by default. As for the Increment, which is the parameter that defines the length of each free-

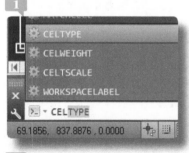

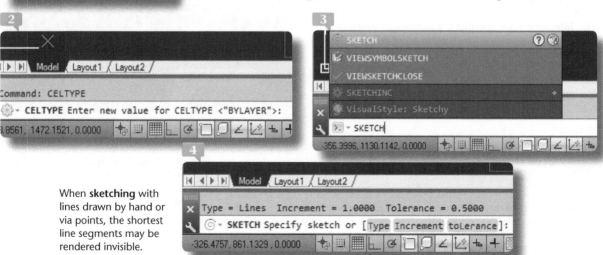

When **sketching** with lines drawn by hand or via points, the shortest line segments may be rendered invisible.

039

hand line segment, the default value is 1. Finally, the Tolerance, which determines to what extent the curve of the spline adapts to the freehand sketch, is set to 0.5. Click again on the **Return** key to accept the default values for Type, Increment, and Tolerance.

5. At this point, if you start moving the cursor on the workspace, the sketching will start. Keep the mouse button pressed down to prevent the sketching from starting and place the cursor on the right side of the floor plan. Then release the button and trace a curved line freehand.

6. Remember that the **Sketch** command does not allow the input of coordinates, and that while using it, the freehand lines will show in a different color than the color assigned to the layer. Click to stop the sketching so that you can move around the screen without drawing.

7. Click on a new spot, draw another curve freehand, and click on the **Return** key to finish the sketching process.

8. To finish the exercise, erase the sketches you have just drawn. By dragging, create a selected area that will hold both lines of the sketch and click on the **Erase** icon in the **Modify** tool group.

9. Note that the Command Line shows that 643 objects have been erased, which is the number of objects that made up the sketch. Save the changes using **Ctrl + S**, and finish the exercise.

To create a line, you need to move the pointing cursor to a distance greater than the dimension value.

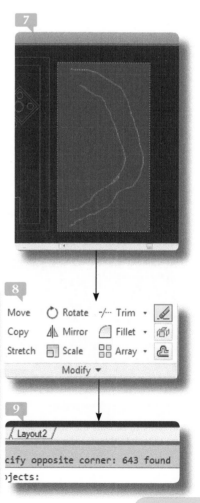

Hiding and isolating objects

IMPORTANT

Remember that you can also **hide** all objects included in a layer by disabling it in the Layer Properties Manager.

AUTOCAD ALLOWS YOU TO HIDE AND ISOLATE OBJECTS, which can be very useful in complex drawings that are cluttered with items. You can find the options to isolate and hide items both in their pop-up menu as well as in the Isolate objects icon located in the Status Bar.

1. In this exercise you will see how easy it is to isolate and hide objects in AutoCAD 2014. To begin, isolate the door you created in an earlier exercise by using the appropriate option in its pop-up menu. Select the two lines that make up the door and click on them with the right mouse button to open the pop-up menu.

2. Click on the **Isolate** option and click on the **Isolate Objects** command.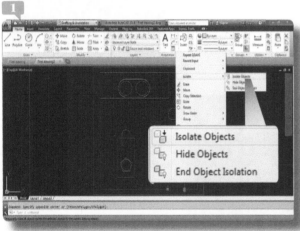

3. All non-selected items are temporarily hidden and only the door remains on-screen. Notice that, in the **Status Bar**, the **Isolate objects** icon is a right lightbulb which indicates that there are hidden objects. Click on the icon and choose the **End Object Isolation** option.

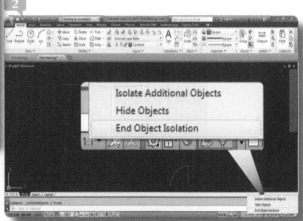

In order to activate the Isolate tool from the Command Line, enter **Isolateobjects + Return**.

040

4. Once again, all the objects in your drawing are displayed. Notice that the Command Line indicates that you have un-isolated 24 objects. 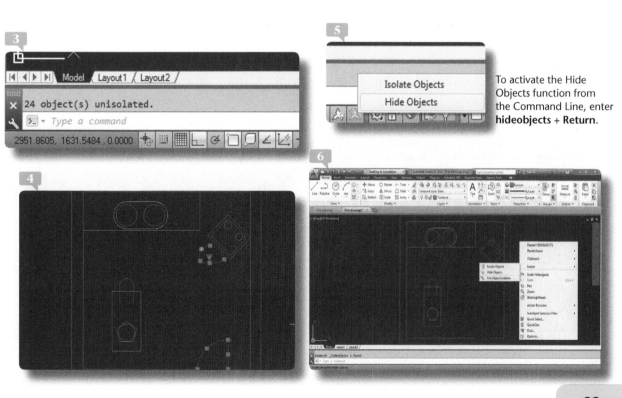 The process for hiding objects is the same. You can use the pop-up menu or the options in the **Isolate** icon in the Status Bar. You can even hide or isolate several objects at a time as well as objects located on different layers. Click on the door and the spline you created next to the stove to select them.

5. Click on the **isolate** icon in the **Status Bar** and, this time, choose the **Hide Objects** option.

6. The two selected objects are now hidden. This system for hiding and isolating items makes it unnecessary to follow them via layers. Right-click on any free part of the workspace, click on the **Isolate** option and choose the **End Object Isolation**.

The two hidden objects are displayed again. Keep in mind that, by default, if you open and close a drawing, all previously hidden objects will be displayed. To change this setting, you must enter **1** for the **Objectisolationmode** variable in the Command Line.

Isolate Objects
Hide Objects

To activate the Hide Objects function from the Command Line, enter **hideobjects** + **Return**.

Scaling objects

YOU CAN SCALE OBJECTS with the Scale modification tool, that is also included in the Modify tool group. After activating this tool, you need to select the object whose size you wish to increase or decrease, set a base point, and specify the scale value.

1. In this exercise you will learn how to reduce the dimensions of AutoCAD objects using the Scale tool. Specifically, you will decrease the size of the three shapes that make up the sink. To begin, select this tool from the **Modify** tool group.

2. You now need to click on the object or objects you are going to scale. Click on the two larger circles and the polyline that surrounds them, and press the **Return** key to exit the Select mode.

3. Specify the base point from which the new dimensions for the scaled objects will be measured. In this case, click near the

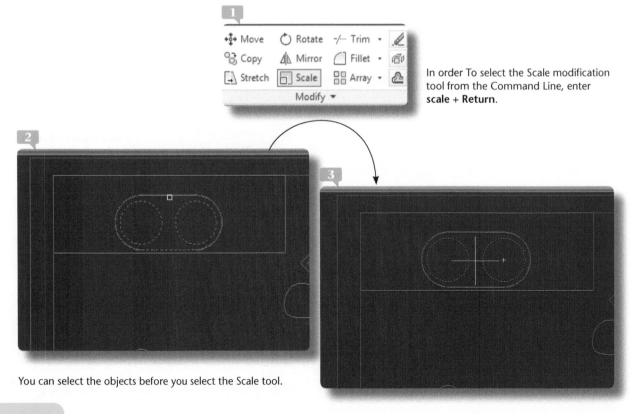

In order To select the Scale modification tool from the Command Line, enter **scale + Return**.

You can select the objects before you select the Scale tool.

041

center of the group of selected items to set it as the base point for this transformation.

4. You can input the exact coordinates for the point that will act as the base point, if you prefer. The last step is to set the scale factor. For the object to increase in size you should enter a value greater than 1, whereas to shrink the object requires a positive value between 0 and 1. In this case, since your goal is to shrink the object, enter 0.85 and press the **Return** key.

5. You can also set the scale factor graphically in the work area, guiding yourself with the preview provided by the program. In addition to the **Scale factor** value, the **Scale** tool also offers the **Copy** parameter, to create a copy of the selected objects to be scaled, and **Reference**, which makes the selected objects larger or smaller based on a reference length and a new specified length. The three objects have become markedly smaller. You can scale any kind of object using the same procedure shown in this exercise. To finish this exercise, save your changes by clicking on the **Save** icon in the **Quick Access Toolbar**.

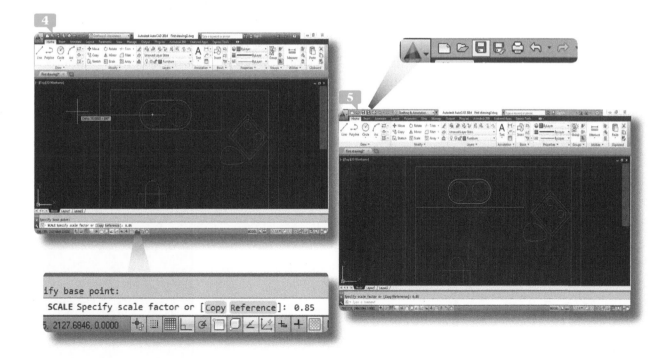

Stretching objects

IMPORTANT

When applying the **Stretch** command you can select objects in two different ways: individually, when modifying independent objects, or by drawing a selection area or polygon to surround a series of inter-related objects. The selection polygon or area should include at least one vertex or Endpoint.

THE STRETCH COMMAND IS USED TO move parts of an object by changing their position in that object. The displaced lines are lengthened or shortened in order to maintain contact with the rest of the object, producing the effect after which this tool is named.

1. In this exercise you will practice using the **Stretch** modification command, practicing with two simple shapes to demonstrate how it works. Activate the **Furniture** layer in the **Layers** group 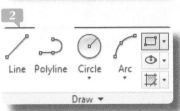 and then click on the **Rectangle** tool, the first icon in the vertical column of the **Drawing** tool group.

2. Type the coordinates **2429,1146** in the Command Line for the first point of the rectangle and press the **Return** key. For your next point, type the coordinates **2246,1343** and press **Return**.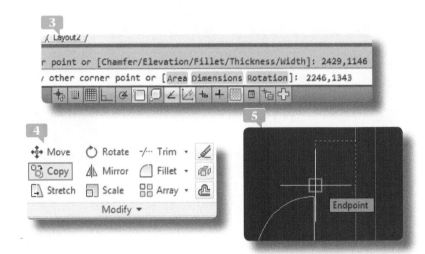

3. Create a duplicate of this rectangle by using the **Copy** tool. Select it from the **Modify** tool group, click on the rectangle you just drew and press **Return** to leave the Object Select mode.

4. You must now set a base point or specify the coordinates for the move. Click on the bottom left-hand corner of the rectangle to place the base point there; next, click on the top

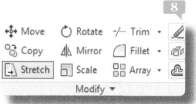

042

left-hand corner of the rectangle to place the copy; then press **Return**.

5. You have now created two identical rectangles. Use the **Stretch** tool to change the shape. Select it from the **Modify** tool group.

6. Draw a selection polygon that covers one of the rectangles and part of the other. Type **cpolygon** in the Command Line and press **Return**.

7. Insert four points to create a figure enclosing the top left vertices of the rectangles, then press **Return** twice in order to close it and complete the selection.

8. By selecting with **cpolygon**, you can select objects that will enable you to stretch only the desired items. Rather than entering **cpolygon**, another easier way to select is to directly make a rectangular selection with two points from right to left.

9. You must now specify a base point or the coordinates for the displacement. Click on the approximate center of the selected group of objects to set it as the base point.

10. Lightly drag the cursor to the left and click to see that the sides of the rectangle that were not entirely included in the polygon have stretched to reach the point where the rectangle that was inside the above-mentioned polygon has moved. Finish this exercise by saving your changes.

You can select the Stretch tool by entering **stretch** + **Return** in the Command Line.

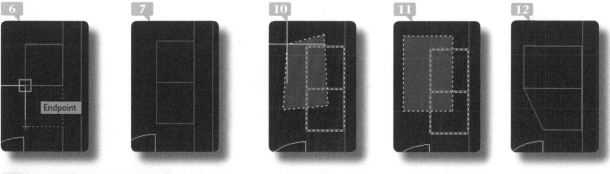

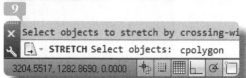

Any object with at least one vertex or final point inside the selection window will be stretched. Any object that is completely included in the selection window or that is selected individually will move without being stretched.

Breaking objects

IMPORTANT

You can use the Break tool for most geometric shapes except for blocks, dimensions, multiple lines, and regions.

THE BREAK MODIFICATION TOOL breaks an object between two points and is often used to create gaps into which you can insert blocks or text. AutoCAD also allows you to break objects without leaving gaps; to do this, you need to specify the two points for the Break in the same location by typing the coordinates @0,0 when prompted for the second point.

1. In this exercise you will use the **Break** tool to create a gap in one of the walls in your example floor plan, which will simulate a window. To begin, enable the **Walls** layer in the **Layers** group selector.

2. Apply an **Extents** zoom to the drawing by clicking on the third icon in the **Navigation Bar**.

3. Open the Modify tool group and click on the second item in the second row: the **Break** tool.

4. The first step is to specify which object you wish to break. Keep in mind that the point you select on the object will be the first point in the break. Click on a point on the upper outer wall in the floor plan, near the left side of the sink.

5. Click on the same line again near the right side of the sink and notice how the line fragment disappears.

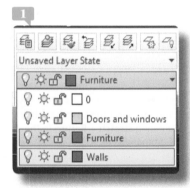

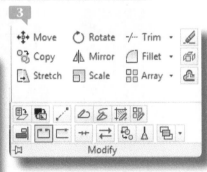

You can also enable the **Break** tool by entering **break** + **Return** in the Command Line.

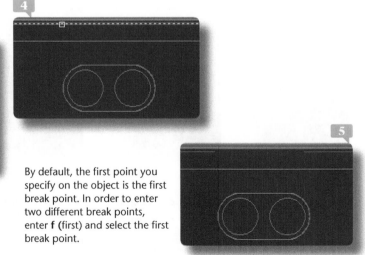

By default, the first point you specify on the object is the first break point. In order to enter two different break points, enter **f** (first) and select the first break point.

043

6. Repeat these steps for the inner wall; however, you should hide the **Furniture** layer first so that the objects it contains don't get in the way. Open the Layer selector in this tool group and click on the lightbulb icon in the **Furniture** layer.

7. Hide the list of layers by clicking on the program's **Title Bar** and re-select the Break tool by entering **Break + Return** in the Command Line.

8. Click on the same points as before but on the line that corresponds to the upper inner wall.

9. Remember that in order to work more accurately, you can apply a more specific zoom to the zone you are working on. Finish this exercise by drawing the lines that simulate your window in the gap you created with the **Break** tool. Click on the **Line** tool in the **Drawing** group.

10. Select the **Doors and windows** layer in the Layer selector.

11. Click on the first point you used to break the outer wall. Drag toward the center of the gap and click to draw the first line.

12. Press **Return** to leave the Line drawing mode and re-select the tool by pressing the **Return** key again.

13. Click on the second point in the gap and draw a second line, tilted slightly upwards.

14. Press **Return** to leave the Creation mode and finish this exercise by saving your changes, using **Ctrl + S**.

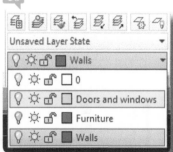

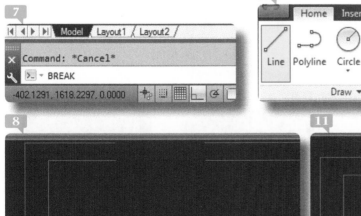

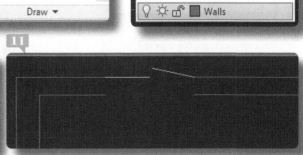

Mirroring objects

IMPORTANT

To place the mirror axis appropriately takes a lot of practice, but mastering the **Mirror** command will allow you to save time working with shapes that contain symmetrical elements such as graphical symbols, buildings, etc.

THE MIRROR MODIFICATION COMMAND allows you to create symmetrical objects by flipping them about an axis called a mirror line that does not appear on the drawing after carrying out the process. In order to define this imaginary line the program prompts you for two points, a starting point and an endpoint. In addition, the Mirror command allows you to choose whether or not the original object should be displayed. As you will see in this exercise, the mirror image is a reversed version of the original object.

1. In this exercise you will use the **Mirror** modification command to mirror an object. To begin, open the Layers list, make the **Furniture** layer visible again by clicking on its lightbulb icon,  and activate it.

2. Let's create a reflection of the two small burners on the kitchen stove with the **Mirror** tool.

3. Click on the **Mirror** tool, the icon represented by two mirrored triangles, in the **Modify** group.

4. Click on the two circles that represent the stove burners and press the **Return** key to exit the Select mode.

5. The most essential component of the **Mirror** tool is the so-called mirror line, an imaginary line along which the mir-

You can also erase the selected items by using the **Erase** tool or the appropriate option in its pop-up menu.

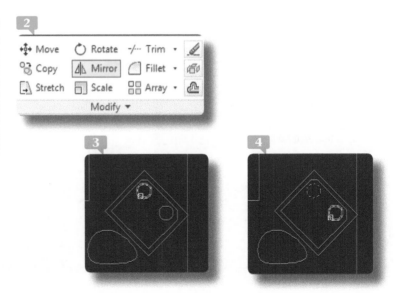

ror image of the object will be rendered. You need to specify two points, the starting point and the endpoint, to define this line. Type the coordinates **2257,1957** in the Command Line and press **Return**.

6. Specify the second point in the mirror line. You need to consider its position in the drawing in order to obtain the desired result. You can view a preview on the workspace before applying your changes. Type the coordinates **2296,1918** in the Command Line and press **Return**.

7. The last step in the process of creating a mirror image of another object is to tell the program whether or not you wish to keep the original object in the drawing. Type **n** in the Command Line and press the **Return** key.

8. When you answer no to erase the original objects, the program retains the original objects in the drawing, and you can see the resulting mirror effect. To finish this exercise, save your changes by clicking on the **Save** icon in the **Quick Access Toolbar**.

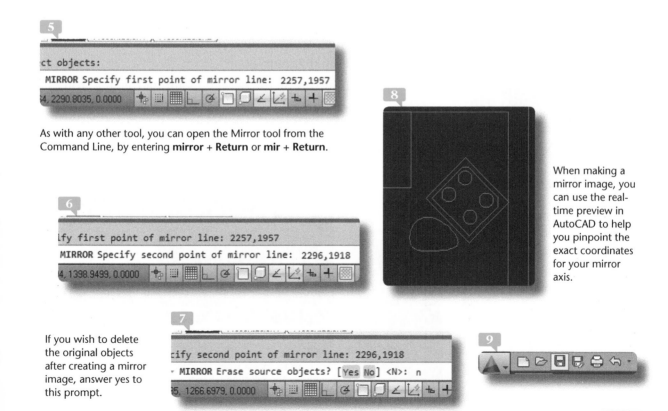

5

ct objects:

MIRROR Specify first point of mirror line: 2257,1957

4, 2290.8035, 0.0000

As with any other tool, you can open the Mirror tool from the Command Line, by entering **mirror** + **Return** or **mir** + **Return**.

6

ify first point of mirror line: 2257,1957

MIRROR Specify second point of mirror line: 2296,1918

4, 1398.9499, 0.0000

8

When making a mirror image, you can use the real-time preview in AutoCAD to help you pinpoint the exact coordinates for your mirror axis.

7

If you wish to delete the original objects after creating a mirror image, answer yes to this prompt.

ify second point of mirror line: 2296,1918

MIRROR Erase source objects? [Yes No] <N>: n

85, 1266.6979, 0.0000

9

New multifunctional grips

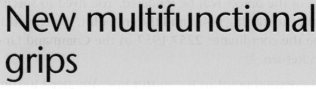

IMPORTANT

You can access the **Grip Colors** dialog box, in which you can customize the colors for the different type of grips, from the Program Options window.

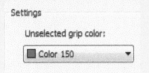

MULTIFUNCTIONAL GRIPS are important design tools in AutoCAD as they help you make changes. They were added for polylines and splines in AutoCAD 2010, and, in this version of the program, they are also available for lines, arcs, and dimensions.

1. In this exercise you will practice with some of the multifunctional grips for lines and arcs included in AutoCAD 2014. In this exercise you will focus on the three items that make up the object that represents a chair. Begin by zooming onto this part of the drawing. Click on the arrow button on the third tool in the **Navigation Bar** and choose **Zoom Window**. 🔲

2. By specifying the two corners, create a zoom window that encompasses all the items that make up the chair. 🔲

3. Once you have zoomed into the zone you will be working on, select the line on the right of the chair and move the cursor over the lower grip.

4. The grips on the ends of the lines allow you to stretch them or to change their length. Click on the **Lengthen** option in the Options menu that pops up. 🔲

5. You must now specify the new endpoint for the line. You can

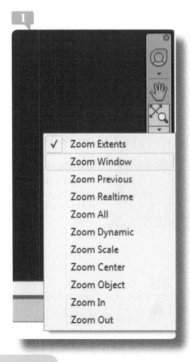

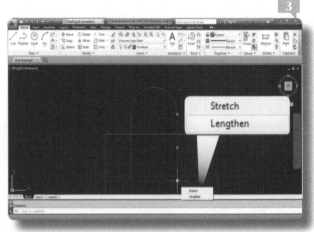

For grips to appear when an object is selected, the **Show Grips** option in the Selection tab in the AutoCAD Options window must be on.

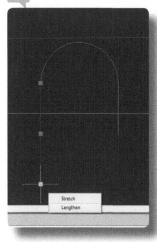

045

do so graphically, by clicking on a new endpoint in the work area, or by inputting the coordinates. Type **1435,1470** in the Command Line and press **Return**.

6. Repeat these steps for the line on the left. Select it, put the cursor on the lower grip, and click on the **Lengthen** option.

7. Enter the coordinates **1315,1470** in the Command Line and press the **Return** key.

8. Now that you have shortened the lines, deselect them by pressing the **Escape** key.

9. Let's try the multifunctional grips on an arc. Select the arc.

10. In this case, the grips on the ends allow you to change the length of the arc and to stretch it, whereas the one on the center allows you to stretch it and to change its radius. Place the cursor over the arc's central grip and click on the **Radius** option.

11. To increase the radius, input **-35** in the Command Line and press the **Return** key.

12. Deselect the arc by pressing the **Escape** key.

13. Apply an **Extents** zoom to the drawing and save your changes by clicking on the **Save** icon in the **Quick Access Toolbar**.

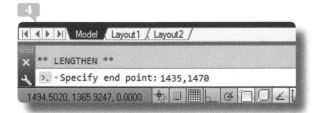

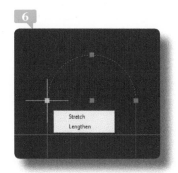

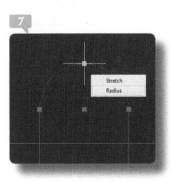

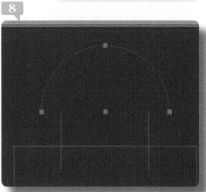

You can set the values for grips **graphically** in the work area or via coordinates in the Command Line.

Filling objects with solid colors

IN AUTOCAD, A SHADED OBJECT displays a standard pattern of lines and dots used to highlight an area or to identify a certain material, even though you can also fill shapes with solid colors or gradients. Objects can be filled in with the Hatch command, which opens the Hatch Creation tab in the Options Ribbon.

1. You can download the updated version of our example file, called **First Drawing3.dwg**, from our website. The goal of this exercise is to fill in the spline you drew to simulate a mat. To begin, click on the **Hatch** tool, the last one in the **Drawing** tool group.

2. The **Hatch Creation** tab now appears in the **Options Ribbon**; from it, you can set the properties for the hatch or its pattern and boundaries, In additon to other settings for shading. AutoCAD has a specific pattern by default along with several colors to be used for shading. To see them, hover the cursor over any object in the drawing without clicking on it.

3. You can view and modify these default properties to adapt them to your needs from the Properties tool group in the Hatch Creation tab. Open the first field in this group, called **Hatch Type**, and choose the **Solid** option.

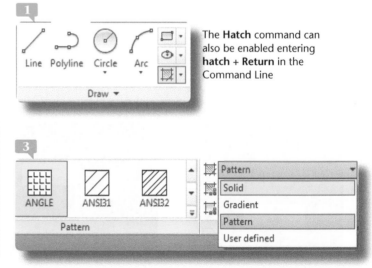

The **Hatch** command can also be enabled entering **hatch + Return** in the Command Line

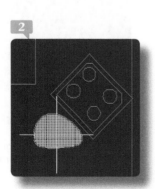

The **hHtch Preview** is a new feature in AutoCAD 2014.

046

4. In the next field, **Use Current**, you can control the selected color at all times. Unless you indicate otherwise, the program will use the layer color as default. Hover the cursor over one of the polygons again, without clicking, and notice how the color is applied temporarily. [4]

5. To change the default color, open the **Use Current** field and choose the color you prefer from the list. [5]

6. Apply the selected color to the figure. Click inside the spline that represents the carpet and click on the **Return** key. [6]

7. Applying colors to solid objects in AutoCAD is quite easy. You can select more than one object to apply the same color to. Try it by clicking on one of the circles in the sink. [7]

8. Click on the **Close Hatch Creation** command in that tab to close it.

9. Delete the color in the second figure by using the Hatch pop-up menu. Right-click on the blue hatch in the sink and click on the **Erase** option in the pop-up menu. [8]

10. Save your changes by clicking on the **Save** icon in the **Quick Access Toolbar**.

IMPORTANT

The **default patterns** are saved in the **acad.pat** or **acadiso.pat** files included with the program.

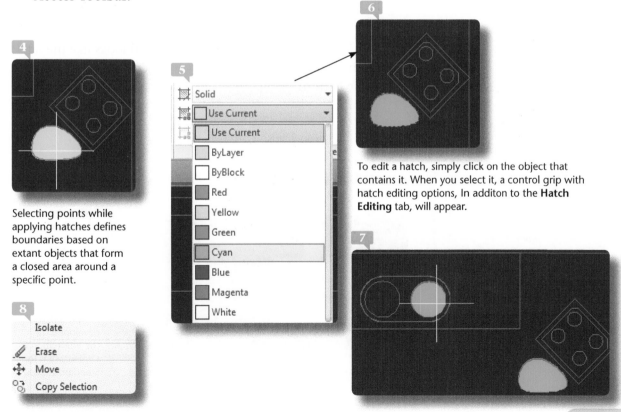

Selecting points while applying hatches defines boundaries based on extant objects that form a closed area around a specific point.

To edit a hatch, simply click on the object that contains it. When you select it, a control grip with hatch editing options, In additon to the **Hatch Editing** tab, will appear.

Applying hatch patterns

HATCH PATTERNS are patterns made of lines, dots, and other shapes used to fill in a closed area or to represent a specific material. AutoCAD allows you to choose from three type of patterns: ANSI and ISO, abstract line patterns that allow you to set standard hatch patterns for blueprints in all fields except for electronic and electric plans and drawings; default patterns, such as those designed with the look of architectural and construction materials; and custom user patterns.

1. In this exercise you will apply a hatch pattern to all the spaces that represent walls in your floor plan. Before beginning this exercise, you have joined the open spaces between the inner and the outer walls with lines, you have hidden the **Furniture** and the **Doors and windows** layers, and you have enabled the **Walls** layer. You can download the updated file, called **First Drawing4.dwg**, in the download section of our website. To begin, click on the **Hatch** command, the last one in the **Drawing** tool group. 🔲

2. This loads the **Hatch Creation** tab, which looks like the latest hatch settings you used. A gallery of hatch patterns is displayed in the **Pattern** tool group. Click on the **ANSI32** pattern. 🔲

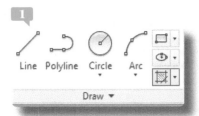

You can also enter **hatch + Return** in the Command Line to display the Hatch Creation tab.

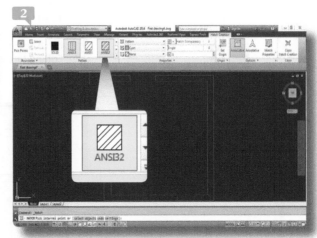

ANSI patterns are abstract line patterns developed by the American National Standards Institute; **ISO** patterns are also abstract line patterns developed by the International Organization for Standardization.

047

3. Keep in mind that the color the pattern will be displayed in is the one currently selected, in this case, cyan. Open the **Use Current** field in the Properties tool group and click on the **Select Colors** option.

4. Click on a dark blue tone in the **Select Color** dialogbox and click on the **OK** button.

5. You can modify the angle and scale of the selected hatch pattern in the **Properties** tool group. Before making any changes to the pattern, hover the mouse over the left wall in your drawing to get a preview of the pattern.

6. Change the pattern's angle and scale. Changing the angle will tilt the motifs in the pattern, whereas changing the scale will make them closer or more separate. Click on the **Hatch Angle**, which has the default value of 0, and enter 10.

7. Click on the **Hatch Pattern Scale**, enter 2 to increase the default scale and press **Return**.

8. Hover the cursor over the wall again to see the changes.

9. Apply the hatch pattern by clicking on the walls and then pressing the **Return** key.

10. Finish this exercise and save your changes by pressing **Ctrl + S**.

IMPORTANT

In AutoCAD 2011 and the later versions, you can select a background color for a hatch. Open the **Background Color** field in that same tool group, which looks like the option None, and choose the color your prefer.

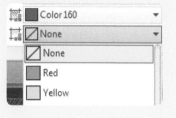

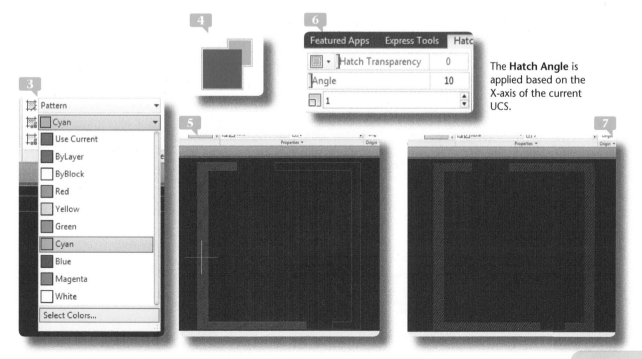

The **Hatch Angle** is applied based on the X-axis of the current UCS.

Customizing hatch patterns

IF NONE OF THE DEFAULT patterns included in AutoCAD are what you need, you can create your own hatch pattern by simply basing it on the current line type. The pattern is defined in the Hatch and Gradient dialog box by modifying the angle and spacing of the hatch lines; furthermore, the program allows you to create a double pattern, in which two groups of parallel lines, perpendicular to each other, are used.

1. In this exercise you will learn how to create a new model of hatch pattern. Select the **Furniture** layer as the current layer and open the **Hatch and Gradient** window. Click on the **Hatch** command, the last one in the **Drawing** tool group.

2. Type **t** for **Settings** in the Command Line and press Return to open the **Hatch and Gradient** dialog box.

3. Open the **type** field and select the **User defined** option from the pop-up menu.

4. When selecting this type of pattern, a series of options are disabled in the Hatch tab and others are enabled to allow you to set the angle and the intervals of the lines on which the new pattern will be based. In this exercise, fill in an area of the drawing and not a specific object; it will therefore be nec-

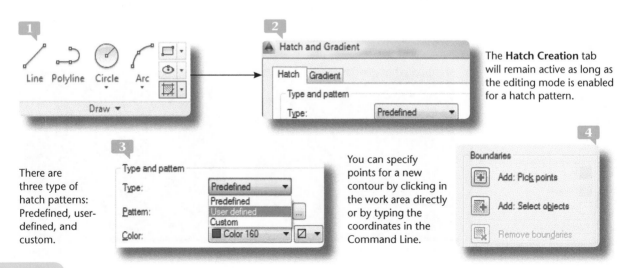

There are three type of hatch patterns: Predefined, user-defined, and custom.

You can specify points for a new contour by clicking in the work area directly or by typing the coordinates in the Command Line.

The **Hatch Creation** tab will remain active as long as the editing mode is enabled for a hatch pattern.

essary to create a new contour. To do this, click on the **Pick points** icon in the **Boundaries** field.

5. The dialog box disappears temporarily so that you can select the necessary points to establish the boundaries. Click on the circle in the object that represents the sink.

6. The program automatically analyzes the data and the internal aisles, detects the drawing area that can be filled, and applies the selected pattern. To return to the **Hatch and Gradient** window, type **t** for **Settings** in the Command Line and press the **Return** key.

7. Let's change the color of the new pattern. Open the **Color** field and, in this case, choose the **Select Color** option.

8. In the **Select Color** dialog box, select a lime green and click on the **OK** button.

9. Maintain the angle and scale. Click on the **Preview** button to see the look of the new pattern applied to the zone you defined.

10. You can now right-click on the drawing to apply the pattern or press the **Escape** key to return to the **Hatch and Gradient** window. Right-click to apply it and press the **Return** key to leave the edit mode.

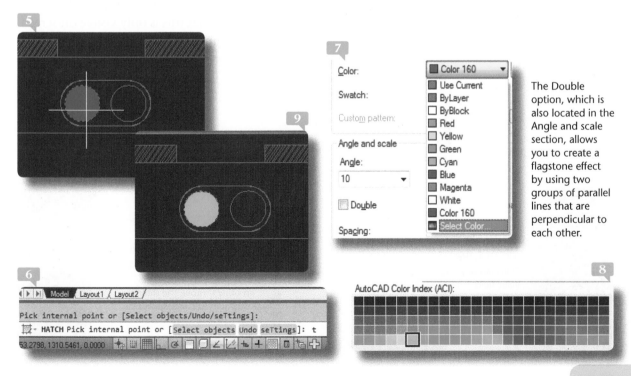

The Double option, which is also located in the Angle and scale section, allows you to create a flagstone effect by using two groups of parallel lines that are perpendicular to each other.

Controlling object transparency

IMPORTANT

Another way To select transparency in plots is by accessing the **Page Setup** dialog box. To do this, open the Application menu, click on the Print command and choose the Page setup option. The Plot options section contains the Plot transparency option.

Plot options

☐ Plot in background
☑ Plot object lineweights
☐ Plot transparency
☑ Plot with plot styles

IN AUTOCAD 2011 AND LATER VERSIONS, you can change the transparency of objects and layers in order to improve your drawings or reduce visibility in areas only used as a reference. In order to improve performance, plot transparency is off by default, which means that transparent objects will only be displayed on-screen, not printed.

1. In this exercise you will learn how to apply transparency to objects and how To select and disable transparency. To begin, make sure the **Furniture** layer is the currently active one.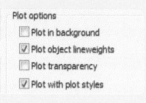

2. Click on the rectangle that represents the table 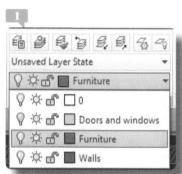 and open the **Properties** tool group to use the **Transparency** command.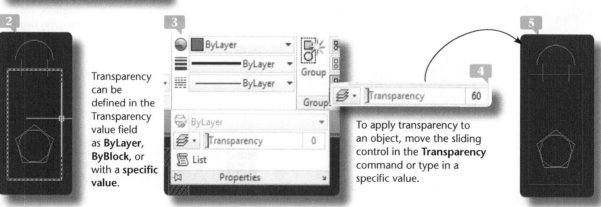

3. Double-click on the field to the right of the **Transparency** control and enter **60**.

4. Press the **Escape** key to leave the Select mode for the modified object and to see how the transparency was applied.

5. As you can see, the figures' lines have become noticeably lighter. Keep in mind, however, that the program keeps transparency on plots disabled. This means that this is only visible on-screen, and not when printing drawings. What if you want the transparency to be applied to the final results? Don't worry; you will now show you how To select it. Open the Application menu and click on the **Print** command.

Transparency can be defined in the Transparency value field as **ByLayer**, **ByBlock,** or with a **specific value.**

To apply transparency to an object, move the sliding control in the **Transparency** command or type in a specific value.

6. This opens the **Plot** dialog box. In order To select transparency management, click on the **More options** button in the lower right corner of the dialog box.

7. This expands the dialog box, displaying more options. Select the **Plot transparency** command in the **Plot options** section.

8. Once the transparency option is enabled, you will see a preview of your drawing; notice that the level of transparency is displayed correctly, even when printed. Click on the **Preview** button. If the button is disabled, choose your printer in the **Printer/Plotter** field.

9. Click on the third command in the toolbar, the **Zoom** command, click on the lower part of the drawing, and drag upward to increase its visibility.

10. As you can see, the rectangle displays the transparency as applied. Leave the preview by clicking on the **Close Preview window** command, the last icon in the toolbar.

11. Click on the **Cancel** button in the **Plot** dialog box to leave it without applying your changes.

049

IMPORTANT

When selecting a hatched object, the **Hatch Editor** tab opens, whose Properties tool group contains a transparency command. You can also use this to change transparency by using the sliding button or by typing a specific value.

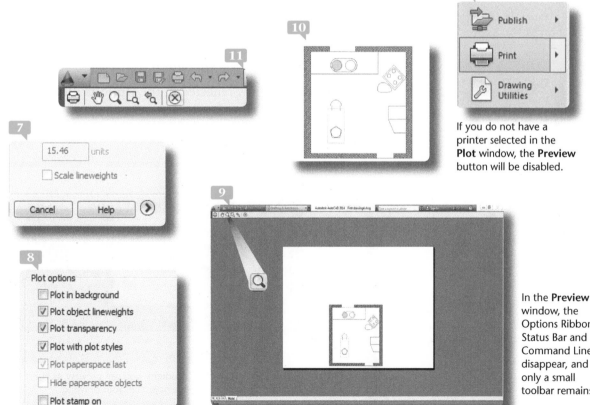

If you do not have a printer selected in the **Plot** window, the **Preview** button will be disabled.

In the **Preview** window, the Options Ribbon, Status Bar and Command Line disappear, and only a small toolbar remains.

Applying gradients

AS YOU HAVE SEEN, AUTOCAD allows you to hatch certain areas or objects on the screen using solid fills, predetermined hatch patterns, or more complex custom hatch patterns. However, there is a third way of filling in objects which, when used appropriately, creates a very realistic effect. This is the case with gradient fillings, which use a transition between the shades of one color or between two colors chosen from an ample variety of tones.

1. In this exercise you will learn how to apply a gradient to one of the objects in your current drawing. To begin, click on the arrow button in the **Hatch** command and click on the **Gradient** button.

2. This loads the **Hatch Creation** tab. Notice that the **Gradient** option is selected in the **Hatch Type** field in the **Properties** tool group, and the two colors you will use to create a smooth transition, blue and yellow, are selected by default. Open the first color field and click on the **Select Colors** option.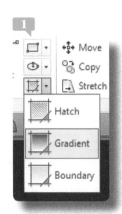

3. In the **Index color** tab in the **Select Color** window, choose a light blue and click on the **OK** button.

4. That same color is now reflected in the **Options Ribbon**. Do

If you want to add a gradient based on a single color, click on the Gradient colors command, to the left of the second gradient color field.

As you create your **color gradient**, you can preview its effect by hovering the cursor over the objects in your drawing.

the same for the second color. Open the field where the yellow color is displayed and click on the **Select Colors** command again.

5. In the **Select Colors** field, click on a dark blue and click on the **OK** button.

6. You now have the two colors that will make up your gradient. The program has nine patterns for gradients, that is, ways in which the transition takes place. The linear mode is active by default. Move the cursor over the rectangle that represents the table, without clicking on it, to get a preview of the effect.

7. Change the gradient mode. Click on the **More** button in the pattern gallery and choose **GR_CURVED**.

8. The **Orientation** tool group allows you to specify whether or not the effect will be centered, and allows you to set the angle to which it will be inclined. Keep the **Centered** option checked. Apply the gradient. Click on the rectangle on the right of the floor plan.

9. Press the **Escape** key to exit the editing mode and click on the **Save** icon in the **Quick Access Toolbar** to finish creating and applying the gradient.

IMPORTANT

AutoCAD allows you to choose from **nine different gradient patterns** that include linear sweep, spherical and parabolic.

GR_SPHER

In additon to choosing the colors, you can also specify how the gradient will be applied to the object, In additon to its angle and if it will be centered.

Gradient fills are often used to improve drawings for presentations, since they produce a light reflection effect on objects.

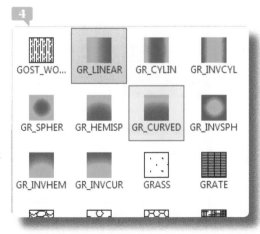

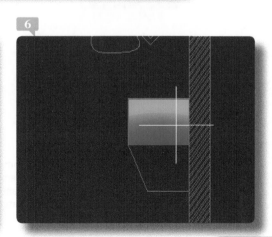

Inheriting properties

IMPORTANT

The **Separate Hatches** function in the drop-down menu of the **Options** tool group allows you to separate hatches properties which have been copied with the inherit feature.

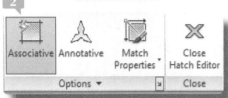

ALL TYPE OF HATCH PATTERNS, whether they be fills, patterns, or gradients, have a series of settings you can copy and apply to new objects. The process of copying properties between objects is called Inherit Properties in AutoCAD, and it is carried out from the Hatch and Gradient dialog box.

1. In this exercise you will learn how to use the **Inherit Properties** command to share specific type of hatches in a drawing. Specifically, you will now copy the properties of the gradient to the polygon beneath the rectangle to which you applied it. To begin, click on the hatch pattern to edit it.

2. This loads the **Hatch Edit tab**. Click on the arrow button to open the dialog box in the **Options** tool group.

3. In the **Hatch Edit** window, click on the **Inherit Properties** button.

4. This temporarily closes the **Hatch Edit** window, and the program prompts you to select the hatched object whose properties you wish to copy. Click on the gradient again to select it.

The **Associative** option is active by default in the Options section. Therefore, if you change the geometry of objects that have a hatch pattern applied to them, that pattern will also be affected. If you do not want this to happen, enable the **Create non-associative hatch** option.

To select the objects or points that will be filled with the hatch pattern after taking a sample, the cursor becomes a box with **crosshair** and a paintbrush.

051

5. Once you have selected the hatch type, the Hatch Edit dialog box appears again, this time so that you indicate the mode in which you want the selected properties to be copied. Specify an internal point in the destination object. In the **Boundaries** section, click on the first option, **Add: Pick points**. 4

6. The dialog box minimizes again so that you can select the object to which you want to apply the inherited properties. In this case, click on the polygon under the gradient and press **Return**. 5

7. The **Hatch Edit** window appears again, displaying the attributes of the selected pattern. Click on the **OK** button to confirm its application.

8. Keep in mind that hatch patterns are also objects that can be modified at any time; you can therefore move, rotate, scale, or edit them. Let's try it by changing the gradient type. Keeping both gradients selected, open the gradient gallery in the **Pattern** tool group and choose **GR_INVHEM**. 6

9. To see how the two gradients have changed at the same time, press the **Escape** key to delete your selection. 7

10. Save your changes by clicking on the Save button in the **Quick Access Toolbar.**

You can also select the **destination object** by typing coordinates in the Command Line.

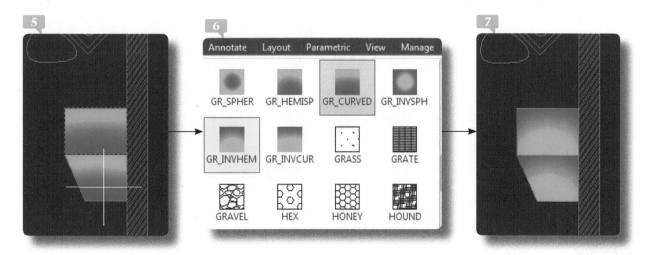

Working with rectangular arrays

AUTOCAD CONTAINS A USEFUL TOOL called Array, which has been improved considerably in this version of the program. It allows you to create multiple copies of selected items in an organized manner, following a pattern.

1. In this exercise you will use the **Array** command to create duplicates of an item following a rectangular pattern. You will work with a new document called **Car.dwg**, which you can download from our website. Open it in AutoCAD. Click on the car and in the **Modify** tool group, click on the **Array** command next to the **Scale** command.

2. In versions prior to AutoCAD 2012, the Array dialog box opened automatically. In later versions, the command has been improved to be more dynamic and interactive. You can now interactively modify the generated associative object array.

3. Select a grip to edit the array. Depending on the grip you select, you will define the number of columns, rows, and spaces between them, now modifying the original array.

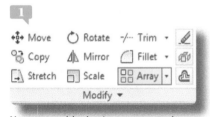

You can enable the Array command by entering **array + Enter** in the Command Line and setting the type of array you want to create.

In **rectangular arrays**, items are distributed in any combination of rows, columns, and levels.

052

4. Press the **Return** key again to accept the creation of the rectangular array.

5. The objects created with the array are associative, which means that you can modify them at any time using their grips or changing the values in the Options Ribbon. Select the Cars array. ⬛

6. This enables the **Array** tab, from which you can modify the main properties of the array, from the number of columns and rows to its type or origin. Notice also that three grips have appeared on the ends and center of the selection, to allow you to change the size of the array and the separation between rows and columns. Click on the first field in the **Rows** tool group in the **Array** tab, type in 2 and press the **Return** key. ⬛

7. This deletes one row of cars. To increase the space between the objects in the array, place the cursor on the arrow-shaped grip located on the fourth car, right-click and select the **Total Column Spacing** option in the pop-up menu. ⬛

8. You need to specify the distance between the first and last columns. Type the coordinates **4750,1375** in the Command Line and press the **Return** key to see how the cars become further apart horizontally. ⬛

9. To finish this exercise, leave array editing mode by pressing the **Escape** key and saving your changes.

By default, an array has a level of 1.

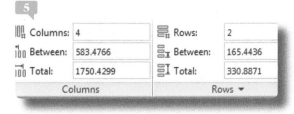

In AutoCAD 2014, working with the Array command is much more **intuitive** because it is carried out directly on the workspace.

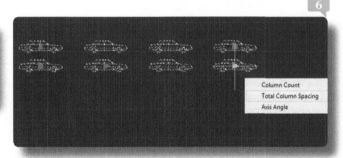

Columns:	4		Rows:	2
Between:	583.4766		Between:	165.4436
Total:	1750.4299		Total:	330.8871
Columns			Rows ▾	

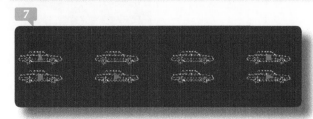

Working with polar arrays

IMPORTANT

The **Replace Item** option in the Array tab allows you to switch one of the items in the array for another while maintaining the interactive array.

Replace Item

WHEN YOU CREATE A POLAR ARRAY, it is drawn clockwise if the value of the Degree field is negative, and counterclockwise if the value is positive.

1. In this exercise, you will create a polar, or circular, array. To begin, undo your last action to display a single object, without copies, once again. Click on the arrow button in the **Undo** command in the Quick Access Toolbar, which looks like a curved, left-pointing arrow, and, in the drop-down list of actions, click on the Array creation button.

2. Select the car by clicking on it.

3. This time, activate the Array tool from the Command Line. Type **array** and, in the Autocomplete field, choose the **ARRAYPOLAR** command.

4. The options in the Polar Array command allow you to create copies of one item located in a circular fashion throughout the graphic zone. For the copies to distribute along a complete circle, the angle should be 360 degrees, as it is by default. The center point of the circle must be specified previously. Click on the approximate center of the car to set the center point of the array there.

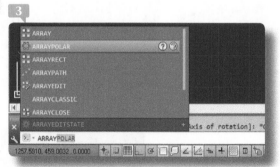

The list of actions in the **Undo** command acts as a program history.

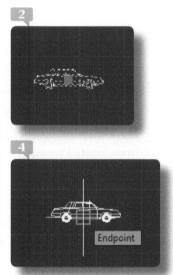

As you saw in the previous exercise, if you prefer, you can enable the **Array** command from the **Modify** tool group.

5. Specify how many items you wish to obtain, which is set to 6 by default. Enter 5 in the Items tab in the Options Ribbon. 5

6. Specify the angle that will be filled. For the copies to be spread along a circle, the angle should be 360 degress, as set by default.

7. You have created a polar array in which the items are very close to each other. Change this In additon to other properties from the Options Ribbon and by using the array grips, but, first, let's increase the view to work more comfortably. Enter **order zoom** in the Command Line and press the **enter** key.

8. Type **w**, press **Enter** again To enable **Window Zoom** mode, and draw a selection window that includes the array.

9. Select the array and change the first value in the Items group to 10. 6

10. You have now duplicated the number of items. To increase the separation between them, move the cursor to the rightmost square grip and click on the **Stretch Radius** option. 7

11. Drag the cursor approximately half an inch to the right and click to specify the new radius.

12. Press the **Escape** key to unselect the array, apply an extension zoom from the **Navigation Bar** to see the effect, 8 and save your changes.

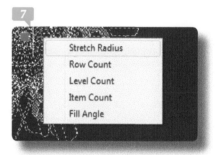

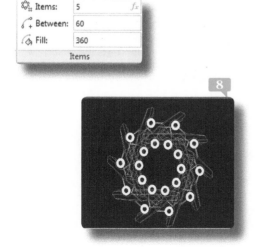

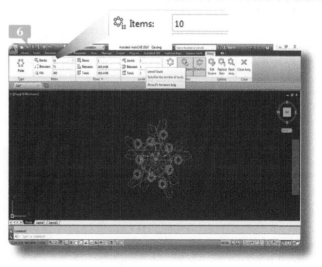

Creating associative arrays on a path

IMPORTANT

If you modify the object that defines the path (for instance, if you stretch the line), the array is also changed so that the objects that make it up adjust to the properties of the new path.

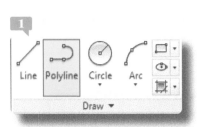

IN AUTOCAD 2012, AND LATER VERSIONS, you can create an array of objects distributed evenly along a path or part of a path. You can do this from the Path Array modify tool, with which you will practice throughout this exercise.

1. The **Path Array** command allows you to spread objects evenly along a path set by a line, polyline, spline, etc. To carry out this exercise, use the **Tree.dwg** example file available at our website. Now that you have opened this document, begin by drawing the object which will determine the path of your Path Array. Activate the **Polyline** tool in the **Drawing** group.

2. For the initial point in the polyline, enter the coordinates **2163,816** and press the **Return** key.

3. For the second point in the polyline, enter the coordinates **3005,1002** and press the **Return** key.

4. Create an arc in the polyline. Type **a** in the Command Line and press the **Return** ket to select the tool's **Arc** mode.

5. Type the coordinates **3750,861** for the final point in the arc and press the **Return** key.

6. To create a new arc and finish drawing, type the coordinates **4604,998** and press the **Return** key twice.

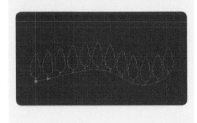

The **route** can be a line, a polyline, a 3D polyline, a spline, a helix, an arc, a circle, or an ellipsis.

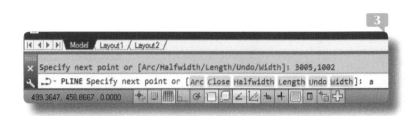

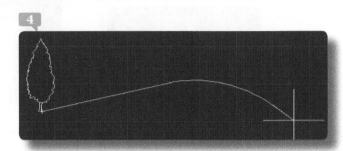

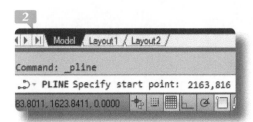

054

7. You now have the items you need to create a Path Array: the original item and the path. Click on the arrow button in the **Array** tool, in the **Modify** tool group, and select the **Path Array** option.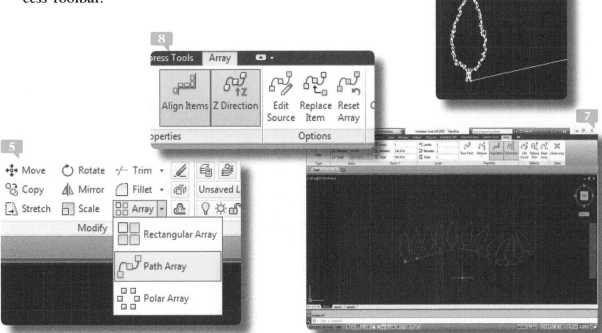

8. The program now prompts you to select the items you wish to spread. Select the tree and press **Return**.

9. Select the path curve. Select the polyline.

10. By selecting the grip you can stretch it and change the number of items until there is a total of 12.

11. For the items to be distributed evenly across the path set by the polyline, press **Return** once again.

12. Finish creating the Path Array by pressing the **Return** key again.

13. Once you have created the Path Array, you can edit it, as you did with the rectangular and polar arrays. Select the matrix by clicking on one of the trees and see how the **Array** tab appears.

14. From this tab, you can change the number of items, edit the original object independently, etc. Click on the **Align Items** button to disable this option.

15. To unselect the array, press the **Escape** key and, finally, save your changes by clicking on the **Save** icon in the **Quick Access Toolbar**.

Inserting multilines

IMPORTANT

AutoCAD does not include the **Multiline** command in its drawing tools by default, and you can only run it by typing the appropriate text in the Command Line. However, if you prefer, you can recover the tool and include it in the Quick Access Toolbar from the **Customize User Interface** window in the **Manage** tool group.

THE MULTILINE COMMAND allows you to draw several parallel lines at the same time. You can enable this command by entering **mline + Enter** in the Command Line. AutoCAD offers a standard style of multilines made up of two parallel lines with a specific separation that can be modified in the Multiline Style window.

1. In this exercise you will learn how to draw multilines in AutoCAD. To do this, recover the floor plan you were working on in previous exercises, which is available in updated form in the download section under the name **First drawing5. dwg**. In the Command Line, enter **mline** and press the **Return** key.

2. The **Standard** style is default in AutoCAD and is made up of two items. As you can see in the Command Line, you can select another style, which you can create from the **Multiline Style** window, In additon to modify the justification and scale of the multiline before drawing it. In this case, draw the first multiple line based on the **Standard** style, while modifying its scale. Type s in the Command Line to select this parameter and press **Return**.

3. Notice that the separation between the lines in a multiline is 20 by default. Enter 60 and press **Return**.

Multilines may contain one to sixteen **parallel lines**. They can be used to represent streets, paths, or other contours made up by different type of lines.

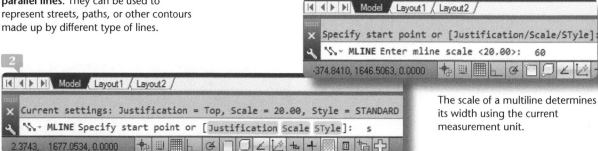

The scale of a multiline determines its width using the current measurement unit.

To draw a multiline, you can select justification and scale after enabling the Multiline tool. **Justification** indicates on which side of the cursor the multiline will be drawn or whether it will be centered on the cursor, whereas **Scale** defines the width of the multiline by using the current measurement unit.

055

4. Justification determines on which side of the cursor the multiline will be drawn, or if it will be centered on it. Maintain the maximum justification option, which means that the line will be drawn to the left of the cursor, and now specify the points in the multiline. Type the coordinates **900,2400**, press **Return**, type the coordinates **900,2700**, and press **Return** again.

5. Enter the coordinates **2520,2698** and press **Return**.

6. Move the cursor to the upper right corner of the map and, when the **Endpoint** text box appears, click and press **Return** to leave the Multiline Creation mode.

7. Create a new multiline by changing its justification. In the Command Line, type **mline** again and press **Return**.

8. To change the multiline's justification, which is set to **Maximum** by default, type **j** and press **Return**.

9. There are three possible justifications: maximum, zero, or minimum. For the new multiline to be centered on the cursor, type **z** and press **Return**.

10. Once you have set this parameter, you can now specify the points between which you want to draw it. Type the coordinates **2520, 2400**, and press **Return**.

11. Set the coordinates **2997,2400** for the second point in the multiline, by typing them in the Command Line and pressing **Return** twice.

12. To finish this exercise, save you changes by clicking on the **Save** icon in the **Quick Access Toolbar**.

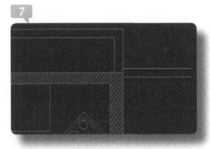

Maximum Justification makes the line appear underneath the cursor, **Zero Justification** centers its origin on the cursor, and **Minimum Justification** places it above the cursor.

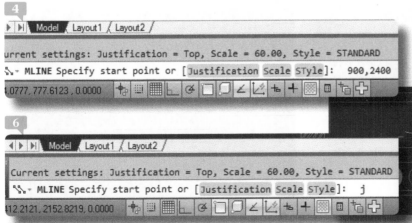

Editing multilines

TO EDIT MULTILINES YOU HAVE already created, enter **editml + Enter** in the Command Line. You can also use the usual line modification tools except for Split, Chamfer, Fillet, Length, and Offset. If you want to use these commands, you will first need to separate the multilines into individual lines.

1. In this exercise you will keep on working with the **First drawing5.dwg** file, in which you drew two multilines in the previous exercise. To begin, move the second multiline to a new point. Select the horizontal multiline on the right and enable the **Move** tool in the **Modify** tool group.

2. Click on the right side of the upper line to set it as the base point, move the cursor about a quarter of an inch upward in a straight line and press the **Return** key to confirm the move.

3. Blend the multilines to give them a new shape. In the Command Line, enter **mledit** and press the **Return** key.

4. This opens the **Multiline Edit Tools** window, which looks like

✛ Move	○ Rotate
○₃ Copy	⚠ Mirror
⬐ Stretch	⊟ Scale

-/-- Trim ▾
◯ Fillet ▾
ᖫ Array ▾

Modify ▾

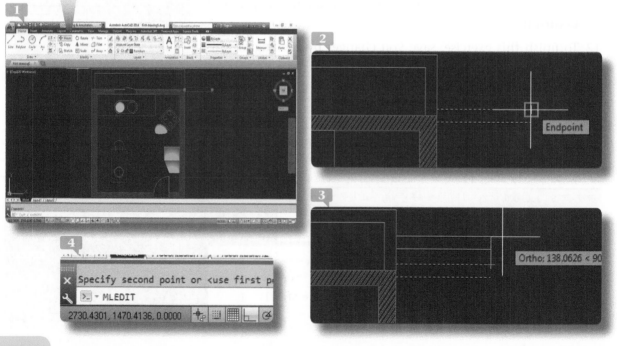

Specify second point or \<use first p

>_ ▾ MLEDIT

2730.4301, 1470.4136, 0.0000

Ortho: 138.0626 < 90

Endpoint

several options to allow you to change the look of the multi-lines you specify. From this window you can add or remove vertices, control the visibility of the tees and the style of intersections between lines, and open or close empty spaces in a multiline object. Use one of these tools to connect the two multilines you created. Click on the **Open Tee** option.

5. The dialog box will now become temporarily hidden to allow you to select the lines that will be modified, as it is shown in the Command Line. Click on a point in the second multiline you drew to select it.

6. Click on a point in the first multiline and see the results.

7. Thanks to the Multiline Edit Tools you have united these two objects, though you must keep in mind that they will still act as two independent multilines. To leave the Multiline Edit mode, press the **Return** key.

8. To finish this exercise, save your changes by clicking on the **Save icon** in the **Quick Access Toolbar**.

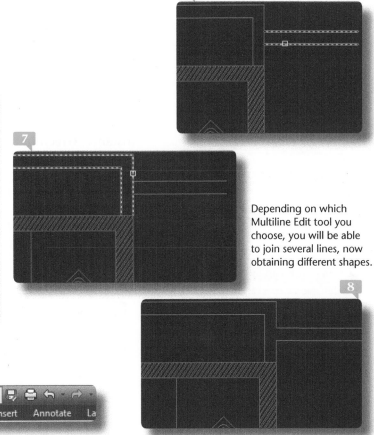

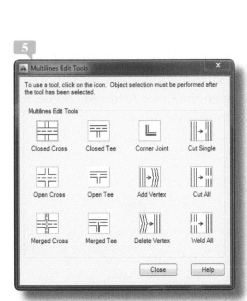

You can also open the **Multiline Edit Tools** window by double-clicking on a multiline.

Depending on which Multiline Edit tool you choose, you will be able to join several lines, now obtaining different shapes.

Creating multiline styles

IMPORTANT

If you can't remember the name of your new multiline style, you can use the AutoCAD **Text Window**. When the program prompts you for its name, enter **?** and press Return to open this window, which shows all the commands you have carried out in your current AutoCAD session and which you can use as a substitute for the Command Line. The lower part of the window displays a list of the multiline styles you have loaded.

AUTOCAD OFFERS A SINGLE default multiline style, called Standard, but it allows you to create new custom styles and to save them in .mln format so you can use them in later drawings whenever you need them. To do this, it is necessary to open the Multiline Style window. When creating a new style you must specify its main properties.

1. To open the **Multiline Style** window, enter **mlstyle** in the Command Line and press the **Return** key.

2. This opens the **Multiline Style** dialog box, displaying the only default style offered in AutoCAD, called **STANDARD**. To start creating a new style, click on the **New** button.

3. In the **New Style Name** field in the **Create New Multiline Style** window, type style1 and click on the **Continue** button.

4. This opens the **New Multiline Style** window, in which you can set the properties for your new style. Create a new style with three items. Click on the **Add** button.

5. Change the offset for the first item. Enter **1** in the **Offset** field.

6. By default, the objects in a same multiline have the same color as the layer they are in. Open the **Color** field and choose, for instance, **Green** in the pop-up color menu.

Keep in mind that the program does not allow you to type more than one word to **name** your new style.

126

057

7. Click on the **Linetype** button and, in the **Select linetype** window, where you can select some of the type available or load other linetypes offered by the program, click on the **Load** button.

8. In the **Load or Reload Linetypes** window, where all available type are displayed, select the ninth type in the list, **ISO dash dot** and click on the **OK** button.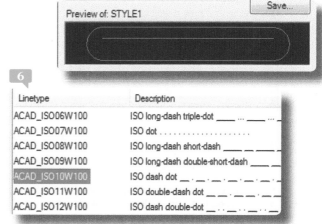

9. Back in the **Select Linetype** window, select the style you just loaded and click on the **OK** button.

10. The **Caps** section controls the starting lines and arcs that will appear when drawing the multiline. Click on the **Start** and **End** checkboxes in the **Outer arc** option 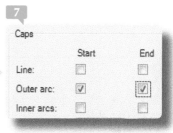 and click **OK**.

11. The Preview section allows you to see what the style you just created will look like. 📝 Close the Multiline Style window by clicking on the OK button.

12. Create a multiline with the new style in the drawing to see what it looks like. Type **mline** in the Command Line and press **Return**.

13. To open the **Style** function in the **Multiline tool** type **s** and press **Return**.

14. Type **Style1** in the Command Line and press **Return**.

15. All you have to do is set the points for the multiline. Type the coordinates **2997,2511**, press **Return**, type in the coordinates **3379,2511**, and press **Return** twice in a row.

16. Notice that the multiline displays the properties you set for the new style. To finish this exercise, save your changes.

7

Caps

	Start	End
Line:	☐	☐
Outer arc:	☑	☑
Inner arcs:	☐	☐

It is important to keep in mind that if you have used a style in a drawing, you will not be able to modify it.

8

Preview of: STYLE1

Save...

5

Select Linetype

Loaded linetypes

Linetype	Appearance	Description
ByLayer	————	
ByBlock	————	
Continuous	————	Solid line

OK   Cancel   Load...   Help

6

Linetype	Description
ACAD_ISO06W100	ISO long-dash triple-dot ____ ... ____ ... _
ACAD_ISO07W100	ISO dot . . . .
ACAD_ISO08W100	ISO long-dash short-dash ____ __ ____ _
ACAD_ISO09W100	ISO long-dash double-short-dash ____ _
ACAD_ISO10W100	ISO dash dot __ . __ . __ . __ . __ .
ACAD_ISO11W100	ISO double-dash dot __ __ . __ __ . _
ACAD_ISO12W100	ISO dash double-dot __ . . __ . . __ . _

Adding text

TWO TOOLS ARE AVAILABLE IN AUTOCAD to add text to a drawing: Multiline Text and Single Line Text. The former allows you to create text objects that will take up several lines, such as contour lines, tables, and long annotations, whereas the latter is used to create separate text objects for each line of text.

1. In the following exercise you will learn how to use the **Single Line Text** tool. You will use it to create a label in a new layer. Open the **Layer Properties Manager** by clicking on the first icon in the Layers group and then use the **Alt + N** shortcut to create a new layer.

2. Enter **Text** as the name for the new layer, press the **Return** key to confirm it, and set the new layer as the current one by clicking on its green checkmark.

3. Before closing the **Layer Properties Manager**, assign a red color to the new label.

4. The **Multiline Text** tool allows you to add long lines of text that will be treated as a single object even though they take up several lines, and the **Single Line Text** tool is used to create a short line of text where every new line of text is

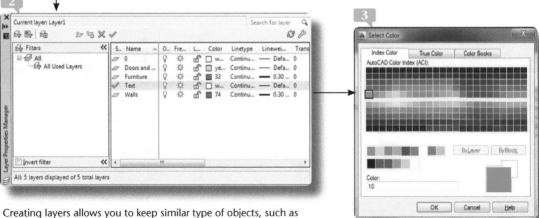

Creating layers allows you to keep similar type of objects, such as auxiliary lines, text, contour lines, title blocks, etc.

058

treated as a single object. Click on the arrow next to the **Text** command, in the **Annotation** group, and click on the **Single Line** command.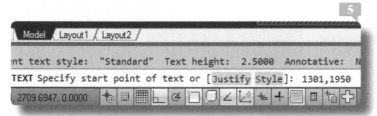

5. Specify a starting point for the text or set the alignment or style of the text. Set the point at which the text will start. Type the coordinates **1301,1950** in the Command Line and press the **Return** key.

6. Specify the size or height of the text. Enter **17** and press the **Return** key to continue.

7. If you want the text to be tilted, you should add a rotation angle. For instance, to write text vertically, you should set the angle to 90 degrees. In this case, you will write horizontally, so you should keep the default 0 angle. Press **Return**.

8. You can now type the text. As you will see, the text will be inserted starting at the point of the drawing you have selected. Enter **sink** and press the **Return** key.

9. The program opens a new line that is independent of the first, so you can continue writing. To terminate the **Single Line Text** command, press the **Return** key.

10. In the following exercises you will learn how to modify the way the text looks, add styles, and create multiline text. Finish this exercise by saving your changes. Click on the **Save** icon in the **Quick Access Toolbar**.

IMPORTANT

You can use the **Properties** window, which can be opened from the **Properties** option in the text pop-up menu or by using the options in the arrow button in the **Annotation** panel group, to change text properties such as color, size, position in the graphic zone, layer, etc.

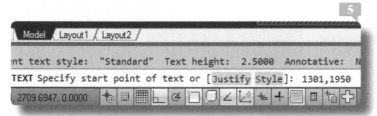

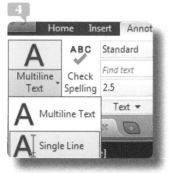

As you know, you can also specify the starting point for the text by clicking directly in the work area.

The **text box** in which you are writing adapts to the length of your text as you write it.

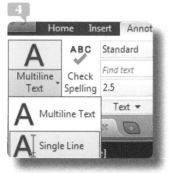

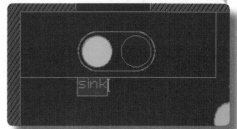

Changing text properties

YOU CAN EDIT AND MODIFY all the text you add to an AutoCAD drawing. In order to change one or more words in the text, you should use the Edit option in the text pop-up menu or in the Annotation tool group. In order to modify other text properties, such as its color, size, position in the work area, the layer in which it is located, etc., you should use the Text Editor tab or the Properties panel.

1. In this exercise you will learn how to modify the text you inserted in the previous exercise in different ways. Before you begin, apply a Window zoom to the text zone to work more comfortably. Click on **sink** to select it, right-click on it, and **Edit** from the pop-up menu.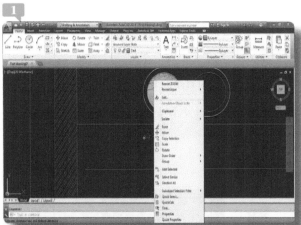

2. The selected word is displayed in Edit mode so you can replace it with another word. Type **wash basin** and press the **Return** key.

3. While the Edit tool is active, you can select and edit text as you see fit. Press the **Return** key again to disable the **Edit** tool.

Instead of using the **Edit** command in the pop-up menu of the selected word, you can double-click on for it to be displayed in Edit mode.

059

4. Change the location of the text from its Properties panel. Click on **wash basin** and open its Properties panel by clicking on the button for the **Properties** tool group.

5. This opens the **Properties** panel, from which you can change a large number of characteristics of any object in the drawing. Notice that the first field in the panel contains the word **Text**, which indicates that the selected item is text. To change its location, go to the **Geometry** section. Click on the lower part of the **vertical scroll bar** in this panel.

6. Click on the **Position X** field, type 1465, and press **Return**.

7. Change the color. As you know, items drawn in AutoCAD are of the same color as the layer they are in by default. Click on the upper part of the **vertical scroll bar**, click on **Color** in the **General** field, select **ByLayer**, and, in this case, choose **Magenta**.

8. Notice how the color of the selected text changes automatically. Change the contents of this text. In the **Text** field, click on the **Content** field, enter **wash basins** and press the **Return** key.

9. Close the Properties panel by clicking on the X button in its **Title Bar**, leave the editing mode for the modified term by pressing the **Escape** key on your keyboard, and finish the exercise by saving your changes.

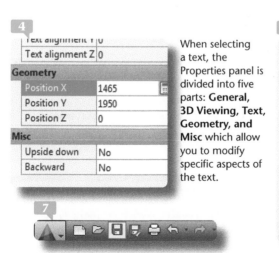

When selecting a text, the Properties panel is divided into five parts: **General, 3D Viewing, Text, Geometry, and Misc** which allow you to modify specific aspects of the text.

If you want to keep the Properties panel open but hidden when it is not in use, click on the **Hide automatically** icon underneath that panel's X button.

Inserting Multiline Text

IN ORDER TO INCLUDE A PARAGRAPH OF TEXT IN AUTOCAD you should use the Multiline Text tool. Once the command is active, you must specify the width and height of the text box in which you will write.

1. Open the **Text** tool in the Annotation group and choose the **Multiline Text** option.

2. The cursor now displays **abc** to indicate that you are in Multiline Text creation mode. Likewise, the Command Line displays the name of the default text style and height, In additon to the nonannotative status for the text, and prompts you to specify the point where the first corner of the text box will be. Before specifying this first corner, apply an **Extents** zoom to the drawing from the **Navigation Bar.**

3. Type the coordinates **2651,1000** and press **Return**.

4. Before specifying the opposite corner in the text box, Rotate it so that the text is written vertically. Enter **r** and press Enter to change the option of the **Multiline Text** tool.

5. Enter **90** as the rotation angle and press **Return**.

6. Notice that the letters **abc** are now displayed vertically. Specify the point where the second corner of the text box will be. Type the coordinates **2741,778** and press **Return**.

IMPORTANT

In Multiline Text, all text is grouped as a single object, no matter how many lines it takes up. You can enable the **Multiline Text** command by using the icon in the **Annotation** tool group or by entering **mtext + enter** in the Command Line.

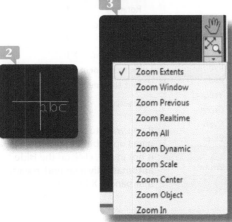

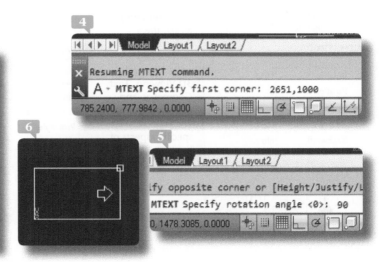

7. After outlining the space the text box will take up, a new window appears in the Options Ribbon, called Text Editor, In additon to a ruler that allows you to change the length of the text box. Before you start writing your text, set its characteristics. In the **Format** tool group, choose the **Verdana** font, and, in the **Style** tool group, set the text size to **14** points.

8. Bold the text by clicking on the command that displays a **B** in the **Format** tool group, and choose **Green**.

9. Click on the **Text Background** command in the **Format** tool group.

10. The **Background Mask** dialog box appears, in which you can specify the background color for your text. Click on the checkbox in the **Use background mask** option, choose the color you want in the **Fill Color** field, and accept the changes.

11. You can now type the text you want to insert in the floor plan. Type **skylight**.

12. To finish inserting the text into your drawing, click on the **Close text editor** button.

13. Apply a **Window** zoom to the new text to see what it looks like and finish the exercise by saving your changes.

060

IMPORTANT

Editing text directly allows you to view it exactly as it will appear on the drawing.

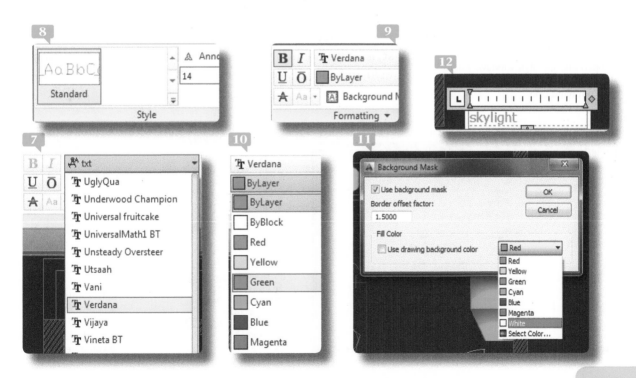

Creating text styles

IN AUTOCAD, A TEXT STYLE is the combination of a style name, text font, height, width, angle, color, and other, mostly static attributes. AutoCAD offers a single style, called Standard, which is applied by default and which can be modified according to each user's needs. Likewise, the program allows you to create new styles that can be used when necessary and whose properties are located in the Text Style window.

1. In this exercise you will learn how to create and apply a new Text Style. Open the Annotation tool group and click on the **Text Style** command, which is shown by an **A** with a brush, on the left of the first field.

2. This opens the **Text Style** dialog box, where you can see the attributes of the default **Standard** style. To create a new style, click on the **New** button.

3. This opens the **New Text Style** window, where you are prompted to specify a name for the new Text Style. Type **floor plan** in the **Style Name** field and click **OK**.

4. The name of the new style now appears in the **Style** field of the **Text Styles** window. Establish the attributes for the new style. With the **floor plan** style selected, open the **Font Name** field and choose, for instance, the **Batang** font.

To open the Text Style window, you can also enter **style + Enter** or **sty + Enter** in the Command Line.

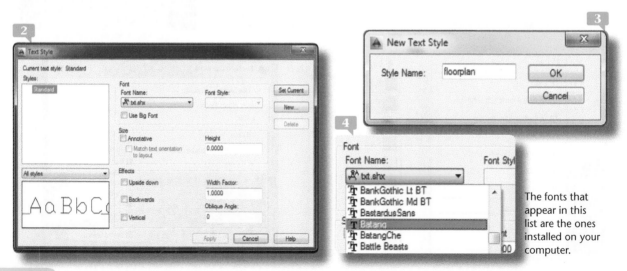

The fonts that appear in this list are the ones installed on your computer.

061

5. The preview will display the different choice of attributes you make at all times. You can monitor the look of the new style before applying it. Double-click on the **Height** field and enter **30**. 🗨

6. As their name indicates, the options in the **Effects** section refer to the different effects that can be applied to the text. Select the**Upside down** option and see the results in the preview. 🗨 Disable the effect by clicking on its checkbox again.

7. Apply an oblique angle so that the text is slightly tilted. A value between -85 and 85 writes the text in italics. Enter **-25** in the **Oblique Angle** field 🗨 and, to create the new style, click on the **Apply** and **Close** buttons.

8. Click on the **Yes** button in the dialog box that appears to indicate that you wish to save your changes for the new style.

9. Insert a new text with the **floor plan** style in the drawing. Select the **Text** command in the **Annotation** toolgroup and choose the **Single Line** option. 🗨

10. Notice that the selected style displayed in the Command Line is the one called **floor plan**, being the last one you created. The first step is to specify the starting point for the text. Type the coordinates **1650,1049** and press **Return** twice.

11. Enter **KITCHIN PLAN**, 🗨 with the spelling mistake, as you will later use it to learn how to use the Check Spellinger, press the **Enter** key twice to leave Text editing mode, and, to finish, save your changes by pressing **Ctrl + S**.

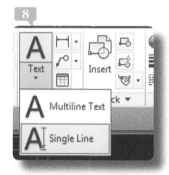

If you need to change Text Styles before starting to write, enter **S** in the Command Line to select the Style parameter and type the name of the style you need.

Annotative text is created with annotational Text Styles, which define the size of the text and is usually applied to notes and signs on the drawing. An icon in front of the name indicates that it is annotational.

Using the Check Spellinger

AUTOCAD INCLUDES A CHECK SPELLINGER that allows you to correct every word in the text included in a drawing. To do this, the program uses a default dictionary for the language it is in. Once the Check Spellinger is enabled, you must specify which text must be revised. If the program does not find any mistakes, it will display a message saying so, whereas, if not, the Spelling window will open so you can choose the correct option, ignore the correction, or change the dictionary.

1. In this exercise you will learn how to use the **Check Spelling** tool included in AutoCAD. Continue working on the file **First drawing5.dwg**. Open the **Annotate** tab in the **Options Ribbon** and, in the **Text** tool group, click on the **Check Spelling** command.

2. This opens the **Check Spelling** window, in which you must specify whether you want to revise the text in the entire drawing, in the current space/presentation, or a number of specific objects. Begin by seeing how to revise specific objects. Open the **Where to check** field and choose the **Selected objects** option.

3. Click on the icon that appears to the right of this field and notice how the dialog box is hidden temporarily so you can select the objects you want to check. In this case, for example, click on the multiple line text box, in the lower part of the drawing, and press the **Return** key.

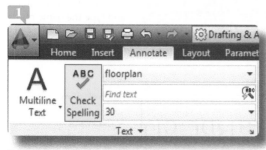

You can enable the **Check Spelling** tool from the Command Line by entering **spe + Enter**.

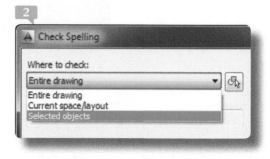

The Check Spellinger can actively search the drawing or the selected areas by selecting several parameters in the new correction options.

4. Once you have selected the object to be revised and you are back in the **Check Spelling** window, click on the **Start** button.

5. Once the Check Spellinging is over, a message will appear notifying you that the Check Spellinging is over and that no errors have been detected. Close the dialog box by clicking on the **OK** button.

6. See what happens when the Check Spellinger detects a spelling mistake. Open the **Where to check** field and choose the **Entire drawing** option.

7. Once again, click on the **Start** button to begin checking.

8. The program quickly detects the spelling mistake (the word **KITCHIN**, with an I) and highlights it. Several correction options are displayed in the **Suggestions** section of the **Check Spelling** dialog box. In this case, the option suggested by the program is correct, so you can accept it. To do this, click on the **Change** button.

9. The default selected dictionary is in the language that the program was installed in (you can check in the **Main dictionary** field in this window). Once the incorrect word has been replaced by the one suggested by the program, the Check Spellinging is over. Close the AutoCAD message by clicking **OK**.

10. Close the **Check Spelling** window by clicking on the **Close** button, notice that the word has been corrected in the drawing. To finish this exercise, save your changes with the **Ctrl + S** shortcut.

062

IMPORTANT

If you are working in another language when making your drawings, you can change the default dictionary to another by clicking on the **Dictionaries** button in the **Check Spelling** dialog box.

Dictionaries...

You can select as many objects as you need at a time. To do this, simply click on them while object selection is active.

AutoCAD Message

Spelling check complete.

Aceptar

In those cases in which the detected words, such as given names, are not mistaken, you can choose to ignore the correction by clicking on the **Ignore** button.

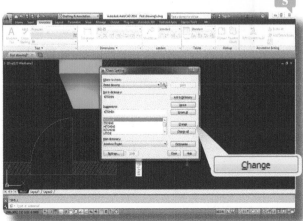

Change

If the program detects a word that is not part of the current dictionary, it will highlight it as a mistake. You can add it to the dictionary by using the **Add to Dictionary** button.

Creating blocks

A BLOCK IS A GROUP OF ASSOCIATED items that make up a single complex and larger entity. Each block can be made up of as many elements as necessary.

1. In this exercise you will learn how to create a block. Keep on working with the **First drawing5.dwg** file. Before you begin, apply an **Extents** zoom. Click on the **Create** command, the first one in the column in the **Block** tool group column in the **Home** tab.

2. The **Block Definition** dialog box, in which you must specify the name of the block and the items that will make it up, appears. Type **stove** in the **Name** field.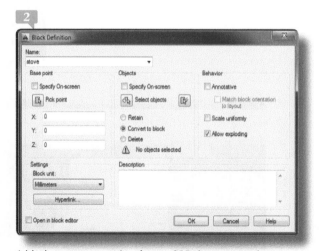

3. In this case, let's convert all the items that make up the stove into a single block, namely the circles that represent the burners and the rectangles that represent the stove top. To select the elements that will make up the block, click on the **Select objects** icon, located on the left in the **Objects** section.

It is also possible to create a block by accessing the Block tools group on the Insert tab or by entering **block + Return** in the Command Line.

A block name can consist of up to 255 characters and can include letters, numbers, spaces, or any other special character, only if it is not used in the operating system or AutoCAD for other purposes.

Already existing blocks are listed in the **Name** field drop-down menu .

138

063

4. The program temporarily closes the **Block Definition** window and displays the drawing with the cursor displayed as a crosshair. Click on the two rectangles and the four circles that represent the stove to select the items and press the **Return** key.

5. The Block Definition window appears again, displaying a small preview of the selected items In additon to their number next to the Name field. Set a base point that will act as a reference in case you want to insert the block. In the **X** field, type **2253** and type **1953** in the **Y** field.

6. As you can see, the **Convert to block** option is active by default in the **Objects** section, and this is the option you need right now. Click on the **OK** button to create the block.

7. You have now created a block, and the selected items can now be moved as a single entity. Click on any point of the stove and notice how all the items that make it up are selected at the same time.

8. Unselect the block by pressing the Escape key and click on the **Save** icon in the **Quick Access Toolbar** to finish this exercise.

IMPORTANT

The **Retain** option in the **Block Definition** dialog box allows you to keep all the designated objects as different objects in the drawing, whereas the **Delete** option deletes all the designated objects after creating the block. Use the **Settings** section to indicate other block properties such as its unity or a short description. When keeping the option **Allow exploding** activated, the object can be exploded at any time.

☑ Allow exploding

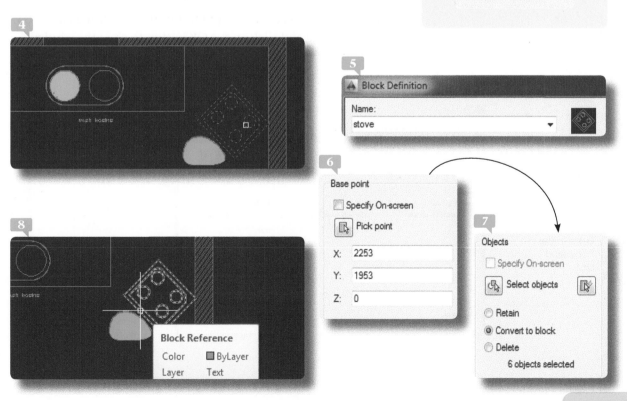

Inserting blocks

ONCE A BLOCK IS CREATED, AUTOCAD saves it in a Library so that you may access it as often as necessary. In AutoCAD 2014, the Blcok Insert command is found both in the Block tool group of the Home tab and in the same group of the Insert tab.

1. In this exercise you will learn how to insert the block you created in the previous exercise. To begin, click on the **Insert** command in the **Block** tool group.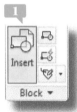

2. This opens the Insert dialog box, in which you need to select the block you wish to insert and specify the Insertion point, the Scale, and the Rotation Angle. As you can see, both the insertion point and the block's scale and rotation can be set directly on the screen. In this case, click on the check box for the **Specify On-Screen** option in the Insertion point section to disable it.

3. When you disable this option, the **X**, **Y**, and **Z** fields, in which you will indicate the point at which you will insert the stove block, becomes active. Insert **1139** in the first **X** flied and **1867** in the Y field and click on the OK button to close the window.

You can also open the Insert window by entering **Insert** or **In** + **Enter** in the Command Line.

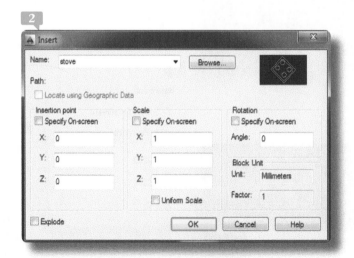

If you keep the **Specify On-screen** option, you will need to graphically select the point in the work area where the block will be inserted.

064

4. The new block appears in the drawing at the specified X and Y points. This simple process has saved you the work of having to draw a new stove by using drawing tools such as rectangles and circles and other modification tools. To rotate the block you just inserted, select it and click on the **Rotate** tool in the **Modify** group.

5. Click on the center of the selection to set it as the base point, enter **-45** as the **Rotation Angle,** and press the **Return** key.

6. Before finishing this exercise, see how it is possible to insert the same block in a drawing as many times as needed. In this case, select the **Insert** command from the Command Line. Type **in** and press the **Return** key.

7. Enter **3** in the **X** field of the **Scale** section, and enter **15** in the **Angle** field of the **Rotation** section.

8. Enable the **Specify On-screen** option in the Insertion point section and click on the **OK** button to insert the **stove** block in the current drawing.

9. Click on the right of the plan to insert the block.

10. Undo this last insertion. Click on the **Undo** button in the **Quick Access Toolbar** and, finally, save your changes by clicking on the **Save** icon in the **Quick Access Toolbar.**

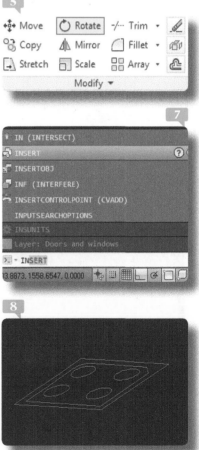

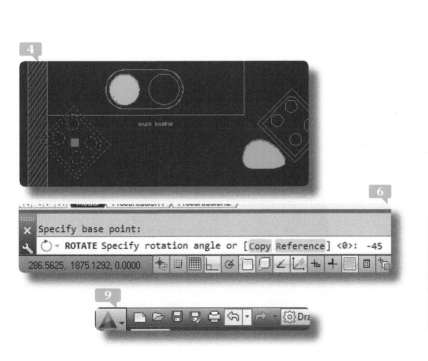

Writing blocks

WHEN YOU CREATE A BLOCK, it is only available in the current drawing and it therefore cannot be inserted into other drawings. In order to be able to use it in other drawings you need to create a standard item, a file type that is saved as a block in the standard item library specified by the user.

1. In this exercise you will learn how to save a block so that you insert it in any AutoCAD drawing. See what happens when you attempt to insert the block you created in a previous exercise in another drawing. Begin the exercise with a new blank document based on the default template. In the **Block** tool group, click on the **Insert** command.

2. Type **stove** in the **Name** field of the **Insert** dialog box and click **OK**.

3. A message appears in which AutoCAD warns you that the specified block name is not valid, which means that blocks are only valid in the same document in which they were created. In order to be able to insert the **stove** block in this drawing you must first save it on your hard drive, an action known as "writing a block." Click on the **Continue** button in the warning screen and exit the **Insert** dialog box by clicking on the **Cancel** button.

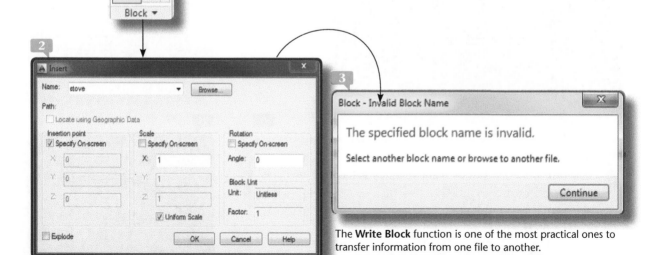

The **Write Block** function is one of the most practical ones to transfer information from one file to another.

4. Convert the **stove** block to a standard item. To do this, return to the original drawing. Recover the **First drawing5.dwg** file, type **wblock** in the Command Line and press **Return**.

5. You can save a block, entire drawing, or separate objects on your hard drive from the **Write Blcok** window in order to be able to recover them later. In the **Source** section, click on the **Block** option button.

6. Open the field on the right and select the **stove** block.

7. You can set the folder and name for the file that will be saved in the **Destination** section. By default, the program selects your computer's Documents folder as the destination. Click on the **OK** button to save the block.

8. You can now use the **stove** block in all the documents you want. Go back to the blank drawing, type **in** in the Command Line and press **Return**.

9. This takes you to the **Insert** dialog box, in which you must find and select the file created in the previous steps. Click on the **Browse** button, locate the **stove.dwg** file, and click on the **Open** button.

10. Click on the **OK** button in the **Insert** dialog box and click on any point in the drawing area.

11. The **stove** block is inserted in the specified point. Click on the **Save** button in the **Quick Access Toolbar.**

12. In the **Save Drawing As** dialog box, type **block** as the file name and click on the **Save** button to finish this exercise.

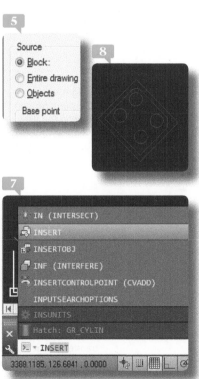

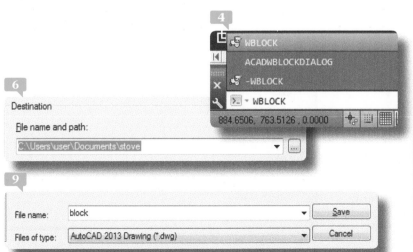

Inserting blocks with DesignCenter

THE DESIGNCENTER COMMAND allows you to copy named objects (blocks, layers, Text Styles, etc.), from a closed drawing to an open drawing. This is a simple but powerful tool that allows you to find named objects in drawings that are not open, both on your computer, a network, or online, and copy them to the current drawing.

1. In this exercise you will learn about the usefulness of the powerful AutoCAD DesignCenter to insert both blocks and standard items in your drawings. In order to access DesignCenter, click on the **View** tab in the **Options Ribbon** and, in the **Palettes** tool group, click on the **DesignCenter** command, the first in the third row. 🗨

2. This opens the **DesignCenter** window, which may be anchored, floating, and, if it is floating, hidden. On the left, an explorer with a folder tree that represents the contents of the hard drive is displayed. You can enable or disable this tree view by using one of the icons in the window's toolbar. Click on the fourth icon from the right. 🗨

3. Another tool allows you to show or display the description of objects, to see a preview of those objects, change the mode in which the samples appear in the window, etc. Click on the **Enable or disable tree view** icon again.

You can access the **DesignCenter** window using the corresponding icon in the Palettes tool group in the View tab of the Options Ribbon, by inserting **adcenter + Enter** or by using the Ctrl + 2 shortcut.

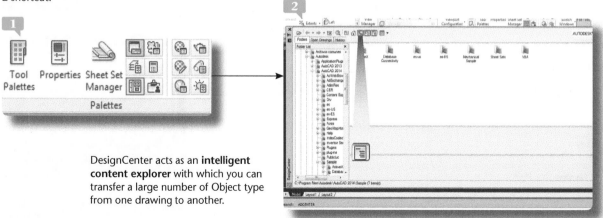

DesignCenter acts as an **intelligent content explorer** with which you can transfer a large number of Object type from one drawing to another.

066

4. The **Sample/en-us/DesignCenter** subfolder contains a large amount of sample objects offered by the program. Click on the + to the left of the **DesignCenter** folder, display the contents of the **Kitchens.dwg** option, and click on the **Blocks** object.

5. On the right of the explorer different default blocks that represent objects you can include in a drawing are displayed. Using the **vertical scroll bar**, locate the **Microwave** block and select it.

6. Right-click on the selected object and choose the **Insert Block** option from the pop-up menu.

7. Keep the **Specify On-screen** option on in the **Insertion point** of the **Insert** window and click **OK**.

8. In order to insert the block, click on the left of the **DesignCenter** window.

9. Before closing this window, see how you can also use DesignCenter to insert your own blocks in different drawings. Click on the **Open drawings** tab.

10. In this tab all the currently open drawings are displayed, including the one called **First drawing5.dwg**. Click on the + that precedes the name of this file and select the **Blocks** item.

11. In the right part of the window, the only block in this drawing, the **stove** block, appears. Double-click on it, click on the **OK** button in the **Insert** dialog box and click underneath the microwave oven.

12. Close the **DesignCenter** window and click on the **Save** icon in the **Quick Access Toolbar** to save the changes made to this drawing.

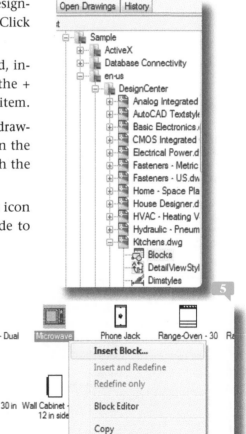

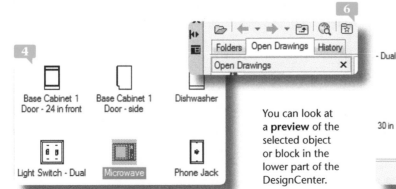

You can look at a **preview** of the selected object or block in the lower part of the DesignCenter.

145

Creating dynamic blocks

IMPORTANT

Dynamic blocks were improved in AutoCAD 2010 thanks to the use of **parametric drawing,** an important innovation in that version of the program.

THE DYNAMIC BLOCK CREATION interface offers a simple graphic medium with which you can edit preexisting blocks, by adding parameters and actions which turn them into dynamic blocks.

1. Keep on working with the **Block.dwg** file, which you can find on our website. To begin, go to the **Insert** tab in the Options Ribbon and, in the **Block Definition** tool group, click on the **Block Editor** command.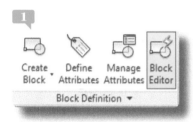

2. In the **Edit Block Definition** dialog box, select the **Microwave** block and click **OK**.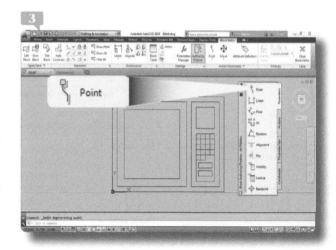

3. The work area is transformed automatically, displaying the **Block Creation Palette** and the **Block Editor** tab. Add a few settings to move and rotate the microwave oven. To do this you must enter two coordinates, one point and one point for rotation. Click on the **Point** option in the **Parametric** tab in the palette.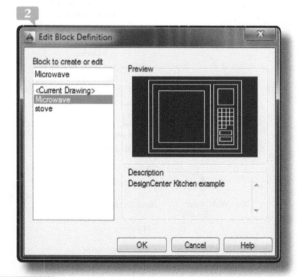

4. Specify the position of this first point. Type in the coordinates **22,16** to specify that the movement will take place from this point and press **Return**.

5. Specify the point where you will locate the tab for this parameter, whose text is **Position**. Enter the coordinates **25,16** in the Command Line and press the **Return** key.

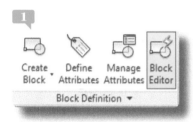

Create Block Define Attributes Manage Attributes Block Editor

Block Definition ▼

You can also open the dynamic block editor by typing the **bedit + Return** in the Command Line or by choosing the Block Editor option in the pop-up menu of a preexisting block.

6. The parameter's descriptor and an alert icon warns you that the parameter does not have any actions associated with it at the moment. Add a rotation parameter, which you will later use to apply that action. Click on the **Rotation** option in the palette, type the coordinates **22,16** in the Command Line, press **Return**, type 7 as the radius for the parameter, and press **Return**.

7. Enter **45** as a rotation angle, press **Return,** and type in the coordinates **25,12** and press **Return** to set the tag for the new parameter at this point.

8. Once you have added these parameters, apply the two actions. Select the**Actions** tab in the **Block Creation Palette** and click on **Move**.

9. Associate this action with one of the parameters, specifically the point parameter. Click on the **Position1** text, select the square from which the label extends, and press **Return**.

10. Click on the **Rotation** action.

11. Select the **Angle** parameter by clicking on its tab, click on the same square as before, and press **Return**.

12. Save the definition of the block by clicking on the **Save Block** command in the **Open and Save** tool group in the **Options Ribbon** and click on the **Close Block Editor** button to leave the Block Editor and return to the drawing.

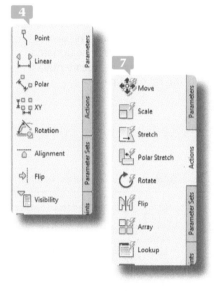

The parameters and actions of a dynamic block allow you to move, scale, stretch, rotate, and create arrays and symmetries in the block.

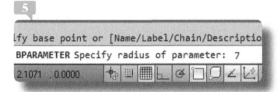

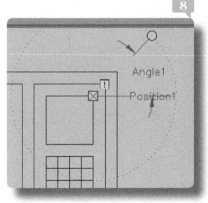

It is possible to manipulate blocks that contain action parameters with **custom grips.**

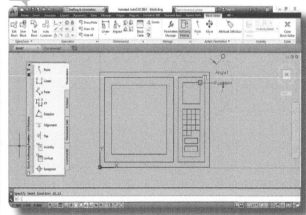

Extracting block data

THE CONTENTS OF A DRAWING ARE summed up in tables that display a list of all their individual components. The Data Extraction – Additional Settings tool allows you to quickly select and extract the attributes in a block.

IMPORTANT

Tables allow you to **link data** from an outside Excel spreadsheet with the information in AutoCAD. The link can be dynamic, so that the information is updated both in AutoCAD and Excel as you carry out modifications. This allows the information to be updated immediately, independently of the file of origin.

1. Click on the **Extract Data** command in the **Linking & Extraction** tool group located in the **Insert** tab of the Options Ribbon.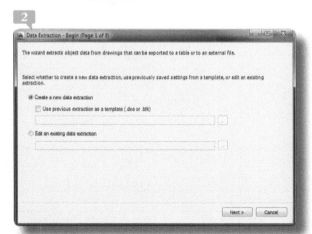

2. The first window in the assistant that will guide you through the data extraction process should appear. Keep the **Create a new data extraction** option selected and click on the **Next** button.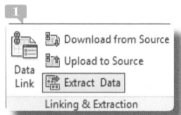

3. Enter **test** in the **File name** field in the **Save data extraction** as dialog box and click on the **Save** button to continue.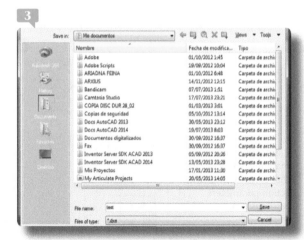

4. In the **Define Data Source** step you must indicate the drawing files and blocks from which you want to extract data. Extract the attributes from all the blocks contained in the **Block** file. Go to the next step in the assistant by clicking on the **Next** button.

5. In the **Select Objects** step you must indicate the objects from which you want to extract data. If you wish to only display blocks or nonblocks, disable the **Display all Object type**

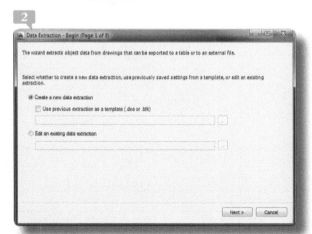

You can also access the wizard for data extraction by entering **atrext + Enter** in the Command Line.

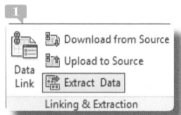

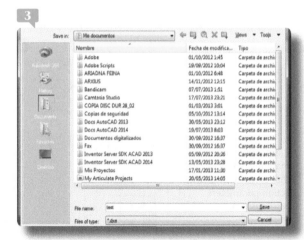

checkmark and select the option that interests you. Click on the **Next** button to go to step 4 in the assistant.

6. A complete list of the selected object's properties is displayed. Disable the **3D Visualization** option in the **Category filter** section and click on the **Next** button to continue.

7. See what it will look like in the end. Click on the **Full Preview** button.

8. This opens a window in which the final aspect of the table is displayed. This is only a preview, which cannot be modified; if you want to make changes in format, you should do so from the **Specify Data** page. Close the **Full Preview** window by clicking on the X button in its **Title Bar** and click on the **Next** button to go to step 6.

9. Here you can select whether the data will be displayed in an AutoCAD table in the drawing, in a separate file in a specific location that you can select with the icon displaying a dotted line, or both. Select **Insert data extraction table into drawing** and click on **Next**.

10. Click on the **Specify a name for the table** field, enter **Attribute table**, and click on the **Next** button.

11. With this page, the data extraction process is over. Click on the **Finish** button, click on the point of the drawing where you want the table to be inserted, and save your changes using the **Ctrl + S** shortcut.

068

IMPORTANT

The **Data Extraction – Additional Settings** dialog box, which appears when you click on the Settings button in the wizard, allows you to specify whether the extraction of nested blocks and blocks in external references will be included, as well as specifying which blocks should be included in the count.

The **Link External Data** button allows you to link data from an Excel spreadsheet in the form of columns to data extracted from the drawing.

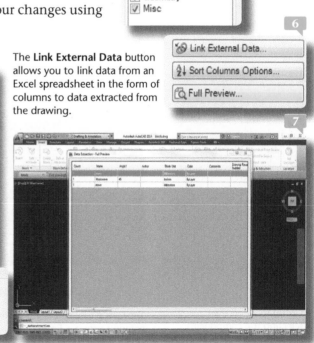

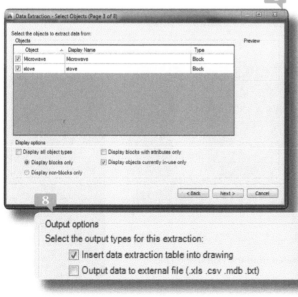

Grouping objects

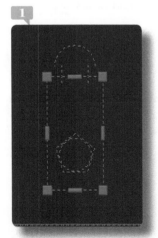

IN AUTOCAD 2012, A NEW grouping function was included to assist working with groups of objects. A group is a saved collection of objects that can be selected and modified simultaneously or separately. The groups therefore represent an easy way to combine drawing elements that should be handled as a unit.

1. In this exercise you will practice with the AutoCAD 2014 group creation tool. To do so you will work with the updated **First drawing6.dwg** file, which you can find in the download section of our website. In this file you have converted the objects that make up the chair and the center of the table into blocks. You will now create a group with these blocks and the rectangle that represents the table. Select these items by clicking on them. 🔲

2. Click on the **Home** tab and click on the **Group** button in the **Groups** tool group. 🔲

3. The group has been created. Select it by clicking on it and notice that it is made up of three items. 🔲

4. Open the group's Properties panel by clicking on the **Properties** dialog box indicator 🔲 and see that the selection name is **Group (3)**. 🔲

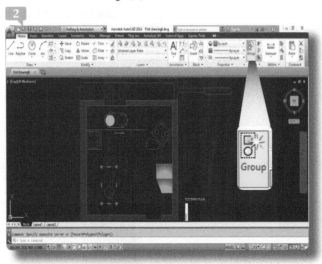

You can also create a group by enabling the **Group** tool and then selecting the components.

The Group tool can also be activated from the Command Line entering **group + Enter**.

5. Close the **Properties** panel by clicking on the X button in its **Title Bar**.

6. Give the group a name. Click on the second icon in the column in the **Groups** tool group, which corresponds to the **Edit group** tool.

7. As you can see in the Command Line, this tool allows you to add and delete objects and rename the group. Type **ren** in the Command Line and press the **Return** button.

8. Type **table** in the Command Line and confirm it as the new name by pressing **Return**.

9. Select the group again and notice how a selection box appears around it.

10. You can choose to display or hide it from the Options menu in the **Groups** tool group. To finish the exercise, see how simple it is to ungroup objects. Click on the first icon in the group column in the **Groups** tool group that corresponds to the **Ungroup** option.

11. You can now select the objects individually once again. Undo the ungrouping by clicking on the **Undo** button in the **Quick Access Toolbar** and finish this exercise by clicking on the **Save** icon in that same bar.

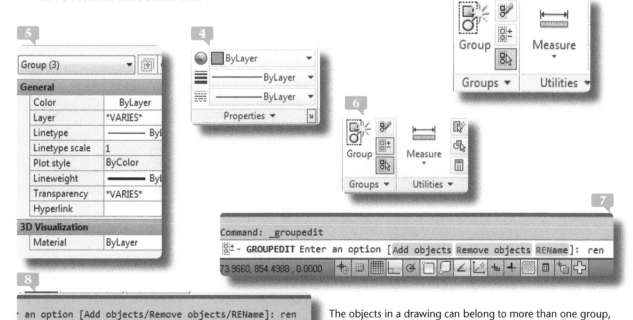

The objects in a drawing can belong to more than one group, and the drawings themselves can then be nested into other groups. It is possible to **ungroup** a nested group to reestablish the group's original configuration.

Getting to know the Group Manager

THE GROUP OBJECTS WINDOW, which you can open by using the Group Manager command in the Groups tool group, in the Home tab, allows you to display, identify, name, and modify object groups.

1. In this exercise you will learn about the **Group Manager** in AutoCAD 2014, a tool that allows you to manage all the groups created in a drawing. However, before accessing the **Group Manager**, create a new group with the two stoves. Click on the **Group** button in the **Home** tab.

2. Select the two blocks that represent the stoves and press the **Return** key to create a group without naming it.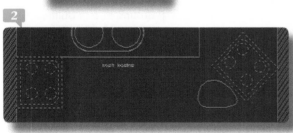

3. If you hover the mouse over any of the stoves or any items in the table group, you will see how the objects become highlighted. 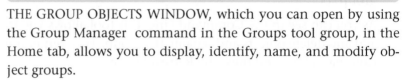 Open the **Groups** tool group and click on the **Group Manager** option.

4. The **Group Identification** window displays, by default, object groups with names that exist in the drawing; in this case, only the table group is displayed. To include unnamed groups, enable the **Include Unnamed** option.

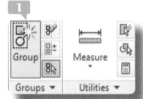

You can even create new object groups from the **Group Manager** .

Group names can have up to 31 characters and contain letters, numbers, the dollar sign ($), hyphen (-) and underscore (_), but no spaces.

5. The new group you created in this exercise is displayed. Select **A2** and click on the **Highlight** button.

6. You can now observe the objects that make up this group highlighted in the work area. Click on the **Continue** button in the **Object Grouping** window.

7. You can edit the group by eliminating components, adding them, reorganizing them, renaming them, adding descriptions, etc. Type **stoves** in the **Name** field and click on the **Change Name** button.

8. In the **Description** field, enter **two stoves** and click on the **OK** button.

9. Open the Group Manager again, this time from the Command Line, in order to explode the group of two stoves. Type **classicgroup** in the Command Line and press the **Return** key.

10. Select the **Stoves** group and click on the **Explode** button.

11. Exit the **Object Grouping** window by clicking **OK** and check that the two stoves are no longer a single group by hovering the mouse over any one of them.

12. Click on the **Save** icon in the **Quick Access Toolbar** to save the changes in the drawing.

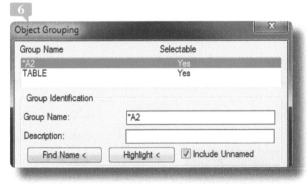

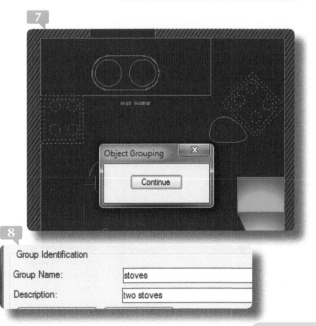

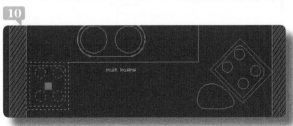

External references

EXTERNAL REFERENCES are programmatic linkages that reduce the size of the active file because these references are only linked and appear in it without being included within the file.

1. Open the file **Block.dwg** previously used. Start by opening the **External References** palette. Click on the Dialog box launcher in the **Reference** tool group, within the **Insert** tab.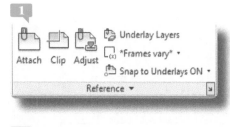

2. The **External References Palette** enables you to organize, display, and manage files that are referred to as DWG, DWF, DWFx, PDF, or raster image files.

3. Click the first icon at the top of the Palette which corresponds to the **Attach** command, to link another drawing to the current drawing. Select, in the box that opens, the **First drawing** file to insert it as an external reference. Click on the **Open** icon.

4. The **Attach External Reference** dialog box opens, giving you access to some variables used to insert links to any file. Keep the default options as they appear to be able to link the reference, to insert it at Scale 1, to specify the insertion point on the screen, without any rotation and in millimeters.

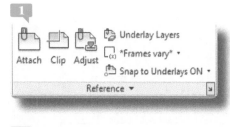

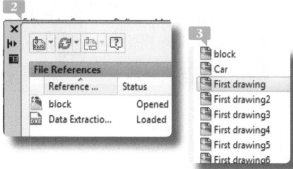

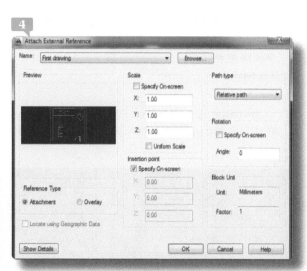

071

5. Click on any point on the screen to insert the reference. Minimize the **File References** window, where the **First drawing** file already appears, and use an **Extension** zoom to see the inserted reference.

6. When clicking on top of the reference, you can see that it appears as a single element.

7. Open the **Layer Properties Manager** in the Home tab to see how the layers included in the linked drawing appear (with the text "First drawing" in front). All these layers can be enabled, disabled, and modified in color, but their drawing lines cannot be modified. Close the **Layer Properties Manager** again.

8. Maximize the **File References** table, select the file **First drawing** and right-click to display several possibilities. Highlight the options **Unload** to stop seeing the reference to the file, **Reload** to see it again, **Detach** to undo the external reference, and **Bind** to integrate the reference within the file, when it will stop being an external reference.

9. Select the file **First drawing** and click on the second icon in the top of the Palette, corresponding to the **Refresh** command, to renew or refresh the external link whenever this original file has been changed, which will be displayed in the **Block** file.

10. Click on the second icon in the **Reference** tool group, in the **Insert** tab, corresponding to the **Clip** order, to use a polyline to mark which part of the external reference has to be displayed in your drawing.

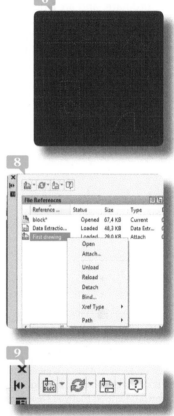

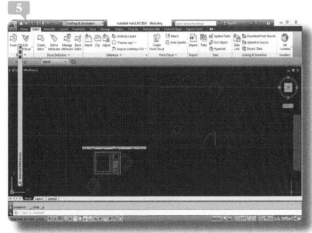

Dimensioning with basic dimensions

DIMENSIONS ARE ONE OF THE MAIN components in technical drawings and plans as they allow you to see the exact dimensions of specific parts of a drawing. The process of adding measure annotations to a drawing in AutoCAD is known as Dimension.

1. In this exercise you will learn how to measure some of the objects in the example file **First drawing7.dwg**, an updated version of the file you have been editing in these exercises and which you can download from our website. Begin by adding a layer that you will name **Dimensions.** Click on the first icon in the Layers tool group, 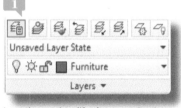 click on the **New layer** icon and assign the name **Dimensions** to the new layer.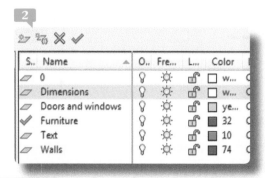

2. Set this layer as the current one and close the **Layer Property Manager** panel.

3. Let's add a linear dimension to one of the walls in our floor plan: Click on the first icon in the vertical **Annotation** tool group list in the **Home** tab.

4. Notice that the Command Line now requests the origin of the first line of reference for the dimension. Move the cursor to the upper right corner of the plan and, once the cursor displays **Endpoint**, click.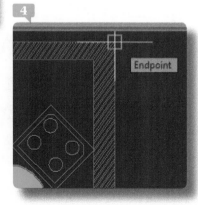

In order to simplify the organization of drawing and the assigning of scale for dimensions, it is highly recommended that you create dimensions in presentations instead of the model space.

All the dimensioning tools and options are also located in the Dimensions tool group in the **Annotation** tab.

Depending on the kind of drawing created, you will need a specific type of line within the dimension; keep in mind that there is a function that allows you to change the line type in a dimension object without having to explode it

072

5. You must now specify the origin of the second line of the dimension. Locate the cursor on the lower end of this wall and, when the cursor displays the word **Endpoint** again, click.

6. The first dimension automatically appears. Locate the text at a certain distance from the measured object. Type the coordinates **3700,373** and press **Return**.

7. You have now created the first dimension. Modify the size of its text. Select the linear dimension, right-click on it, and choose the **Properties** option.

8. In the **Properties** field, click on the lower part of the **vertical scroll bar** on the left until you locate the **Text** section, click on the **Text height** field and change the value to **50**.

9. Close the **Properties** panel and see how the size of the text in the dimension has increased.

10. Add a second dimension to indicate the width of the sink. In this case, select the **Linear** tool from the Command Line by entering **dimlinear** and press the **Return** key.

11. Type the coordinates **2379,1724** in the Command Line, press the **Return** key, type the coordinates **2793,1724**, and press the **Return** key again.

12. To locate the second dimension in the drawing, move the cursor half a centimeter down and click.

13. Save your changes by clicking on the **Save** icon in the **Quick Access Toolbar**.

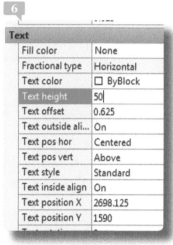

Text	
Fill color	None
Fractional type	Horizontal
Text color	☐ ByBlock
Text height	50
Text offset	0.625
Text outside ali...	On
Text pos hor	Centered
Text pos vert	Above
Text style	Standard
Text inside align	On
Text position X	2698.125
Text position Y	1590

All dimensions are **associative**; therefore, if geometric changes are made to the object, the dimension will also change its values.

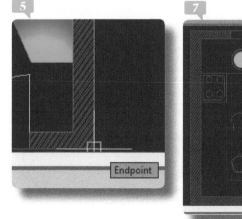

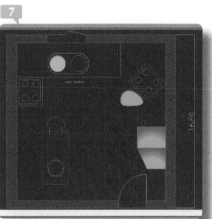

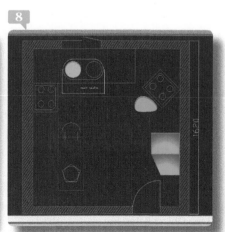

Using radius and diameter dimensions

EVEN THOUGH LINEAR DIMENSIONS are the most frequently used ones, AutoCAD also includes radius, diameter, and angle dimensions. The first two type are used to indicate the length of an arc or circle, keeping in mind the dimension that is to be measured rather than the object type. Radius and diameter dimensions work almost exactly the same and are controlled in the same way.

1. In this exercise you will create a radius and a diameter dimension. To do this, continue working on the **First drawing7.dwg** file. To begin, enable the **Presentation1** view by clicking on its tab and then apply a **Zoom W**indow to the area of the sink. (You can enable this zoom from the **Navigation Bar.**)

2. In the **Annotation** tool group in the **Home** tab of the **Options Ribbon**, open the Linear command and click on the **Radius** command.

3. This command allows you to create a radius dimension on a circle or arc. As you can see, the Command Line prompts you to specify an arc or circle whose radius you want to dimension. Click on the circle on the left in the sink.

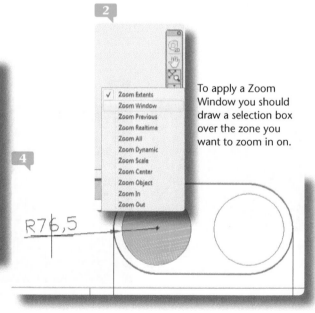

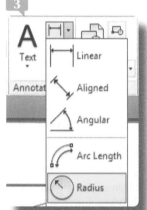

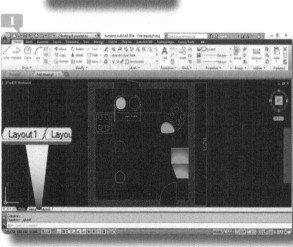

To apply a Zoom Window you should draw a selection box over the zone you want to zoom in on.

In order to work with maximum precision in the drawing area, keep **Object Reference** mode enabled.

073

4. The measurement of circle's radius is automatically displayed. To make it clear that the figure displayed by this dimension is the length of a radius, the letter **R** is displayed in front of its numerical value. To locate the dimension on the drawing and see it better, type the coordinates **86,146** in the Command Line and press the **Return** key.

5. You can use the **Diameter** command in a similar fashion, and it is used to calculate the length of the diameter of an arc or a circle. Open the **Radius** command in the **Annotation** tool group and, this time, choose the **Diameter** command. 💬

6. You must now specify the arc or circle whose diameter you wish to obtain. Click on the circle on the right in the sink and notice how the requested figure appears. 💬

7. In this case, the numerical value for the diameter is accompanied by a symbol displaying a circle and a line that crosses it. Move the cursor toward the right until you touch the right side of the circle and click for the dimension to stay inside the shape. 💬

8. As you can see, adding dimensions is very easy and it allows you to display basic information in the drawing in some cases. Finish this exercise by clicking on the **Save** icon in the **Quick Access Toolbar** to save your changes.

IMPORTANT

Once you have located the dimension on the drawing, you can select it by clicking on it and use its **grips** to relocate it easily. In this new version of AutoCAD, these grips allow you to add continuous and base line dimensions, to invert the location of the cursor, and to control the location of the text in the dimension.

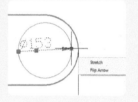

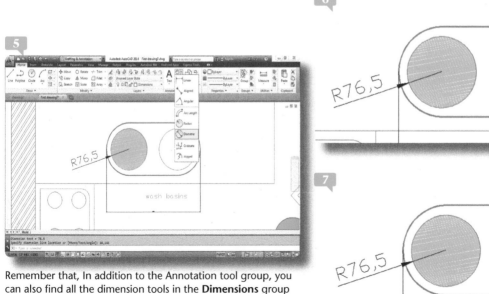

Remember that, In addition to the Annotation tool group, you can also find all the dimension tools in the **Dimensions** group in the **Annotation** tab.

Using angular dimensions

THE ANGULAR DIMENSION TOOL allows you to create a dimension that measures the angle between two lines or the angle described by an arc segment. The angular dimension uses angles in the dimension text instead of linear dimensions.

1. In this exercise you will learn about the usefulness of the Angular Dimension Annotation tool, with which you will annotate an angle in your **First drawing7.dwg** plan. Begin by applying an **Extents** zoom, from the **Navigation Bar**, to the zone that you will be working with. 🔲

2. Use the **Zoom Window** on that same bar and apply a zoom of this type on the door zone, on the lower right corner of the plan. 🔲

3. Open the **Diameter** command in the **Annotation** tool group and click on the **Angular** option. 🔲

4. The Command Line now prompts you to select an arc, circle, line, or vertex. Click on the yellow arc that represents the door opening.

The Angular Dimension tool can be enabled from the Command Line by entering **dimangle + Enter**.

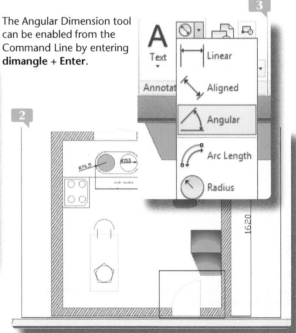

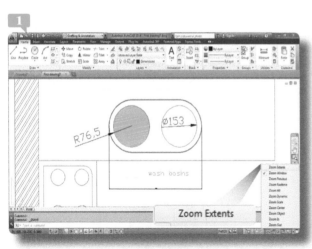

Remember that an **Extents zoom** is applied directly to the drawing without having to click on a specific spot.

074

5. The dimension automatically appears. 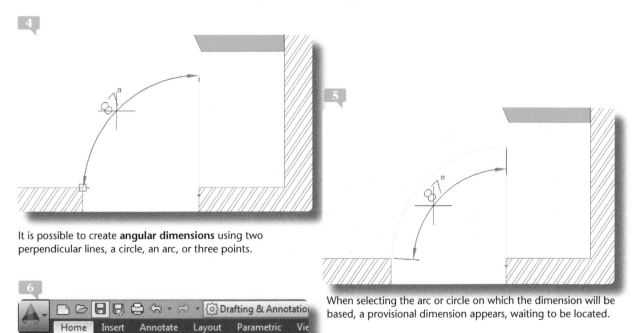 You must now specify the location of the arc for the dimension line. Drag the cursor down and click approximately half a centimeter away from the arc to locate the annotation there.

6. Keep in mind that, when dimensioning the angle between two lines, the Command Line will logically prompt you to specify two lines. Angular dimensions can measure a specific quadrant formed when dimensioning the angle between the ends of a line or arc, the center of a circle, or two vertices. As you create an angular dimension, four possible angles can be measured. Specifying a quadrant guarantees that you are dimensioning the correct angle. When placing an angular dimension after specifying the quadrant, the dimension text can be placed outside the reference lines of the dimension. The dimension line is expanded automatically. If straight and nonparallel lines are used to specify an angle, the dimension line arc will extend between both lines. If the dimension line arc does not meet one or both of the lines it is dimensioning, the program draws one or two reference lines that intersect the dimension line arc. The arc is always less than 180 degrees. In the following exercises you will continue practicing with other dimension options. To finish this exercise, click on the **Save** button in the **Quick Access Toolbar**.

It is possible to create **angular dimensions** using two perpendicular lines, a circle, an arc, or three points.

When selecting the arc or circle on which the dimension will be based, a provisional dimension appears, waiting to be located.

Adding jogs to dimensions

IMPORTANT

For an arc dimension to be correct, the **radial dimension** must go through its center. However, in many cases, the size of the drawing puts the center outside the plan, which forced you to decompose the radial dimension and edit it manually in earlier versions of AutoCAD.

THE JOG COMMAND allows you to specify a jog angle to correctly dimension large curves whose center cannot be seen in its true position, without having to undo the dimension. These dimensions measure the radius of the object and display the dimension text with a radius symbol.

1. In this exercise you will learn about the usefulness of the **Jogged** dimension tool. Apply an **Extents** zoom to the drawing.

2. Click on the **Zoom** command in the **Navigation Bar** again and click on the **Zoom Window** option.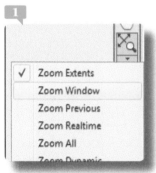

3. Once the window is active, select the corners of the zoom window. Type the coordinates **91,106** and press **Return**.

4. Type the coordinates **100,96** to locate the second corner of the selection window in this point and press enter to see that the drawing zone appears larger on the screen.

5. The center of the arc, which represents the back of the chair, is outside of your view, so you can use the **Jogged** tool to create the radius dimension. Open the **Angular** command in the **Annotation** tool group and choose the **Jogged** option.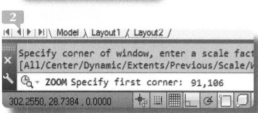

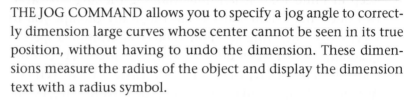

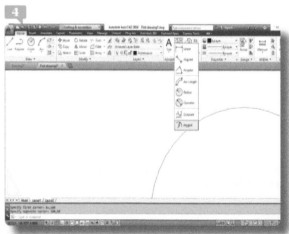

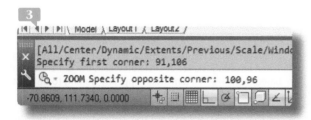

You can also access the Jogged command by entering **dimjogline + Enter** order in the Command Line.

075

6. The first thing the program prompts you for is to specify the object to which you want to add the jog line. Click on the approximate half of the arc, which is currently visible, to select it.

7. Specify the point of origin for the dimension in the desired location. Enter the coordinates **103,97** in the Command Line and press **Return**.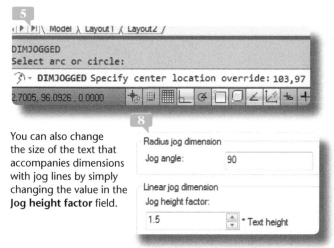

8. The text and dimension line appear automatically. Using the options displayed in the Command Line, you can locate the line, modify the text, or change the angle in which it is displayed. Type the coordinates **106,97** and press **Return**.

9. The only step that remains is to specify the location of the jog line. Type the coordinates **109,103** and press **Return.**

10. Apply an **Extent** zoom to the drawing again to see the results.

11. Open the **Dimension Style Manager** window from which you can modify the main characteristics of the dimension style you are working with. Open the **Annotation** tool group and click on the **Dimension style** icon which is represented by a line with arrows on each end and a brush.

12. The **Dimension Style Manager** displays the default **ISO-25** style. Change some of its characteristics. Click on the **Modify** button.

13. Select the **Symbols and Arrows** tab in the **Modify Dimension Style** window, change the **Jog angle** value to **90** and click **OK**.

14. Click on **Close** in the **Dimension Style Manager** and save your changes.

IMPORTANT

The advantage of working with jog lines is that the point of origin of the dimension can be specified in a more practical location, known as **center replacement location**.

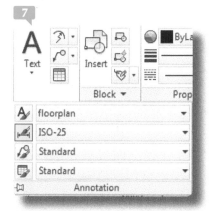

Changes carried out in the **Dimension Style Manager** are only applied to dimensions created from that moment onwards.

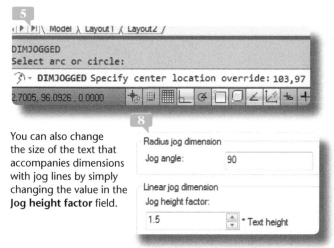

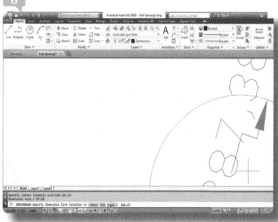

You can also change the size of the text that accompanies dimensions with jog lines by simply changing the value in the **Jog height factor** field.

Radius jog dimension
Jog angle: 90

Linear jog dimension
Jog height factor:
1.5   * Text height

Dimensioning arc lengths

AUTOCAD INCLUDES A DIMENSIONING tool that allows you to measure the distance of the segment of a polyline arc or an arc: the Arc Length command. To separate arc length dimensions from linear or angular dimensions, the former display an arc symbol by default.

1. In this exercise you will use the **Arc Length** command to measure the arc of the door in your floor plan. Apply a **Zoom Window** on that area of the drawing, select the drop-down menu from the first icon in the vertical list in the **Annotation** tool group and click on the **Arc Length** option.

2. Select the arc to be dimensioned. Click on the arc that represents the opening of the door.

3. The dimension text appears automatically. You need to specify its location. Type the coordinates **165,51** and press **Return**.

4. Notice that the program automatically adds an arc in front of the dimension text to distinguish this type of dimension from linear and angular dimensions. AutoCAD allows you to change the location of the symbol or even to omit it. Click on the new dimension to select it.

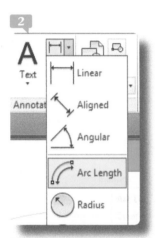

It is also possible To select this tool entering **dimarc** + **Return** in the Command Line.

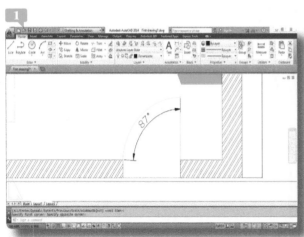

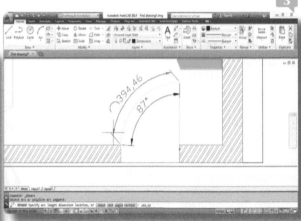

If you prefer, you can locate the dimension graphically on the drawing area by clicking on the point you want.

076

5. Open the drop-down menu in the **Annotation** tool group and click on the **Dimension style** icon.

6. This opens the **Dimension Style Manager**, with which you worked in a previous exercise. With the current style, **ISO-25**, selected, click on the **Modify** button.

7. The **Arc length symbol** section in the **Symbols and Arrows** tab allows you to locate the arc in front of the dimension text, an option that is active by default, or on it. If you enable the **None** option, the symbol that identifies arc length dimensions will not be displayed. Select the **Above dimension text** option and click on the **OK** button to apply the change.

8. Close the **Dimension Style Manager** window by clicking on the **Close** button and notice how the dimension symbol is now above the numerical value.

9. You can modify the main attributes in a dimension without affecting the other dimensions in the drawing from the Properties panel. Click on the arc length dimension again to select it, open its pop-up menu, and choose the **Properties** option.

10. Click on **Color** in the **General** section of the **Properties** panel.

11. Open the **Color** field and select **Red** from the list.

12. The change is applied to the dimension instantly. Close the **Properties** panel by clicking on the X button in its **Title Bar**, press the **Escape** key to unselect the **Access Toolbar** and save your changes by clicking on the **Save** icon in the **Quick Access Toolbar**.

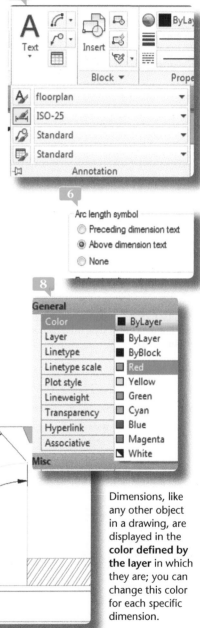

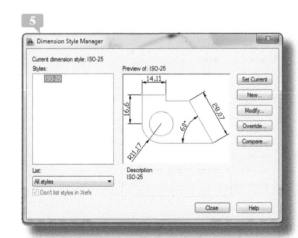

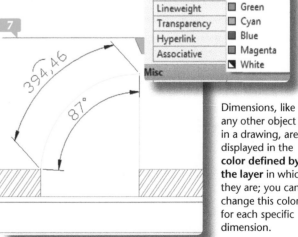

Dimensions, like any other object in a drawing, are displayed in the **color defined by the layer** in which they are; you can change this color for each specific dimension.

Inserting baseline dimensions

IMPORTANT

AutoCAD stacks baseline annotations with an incremental height, which you can modify in the Lines tab in the **Modify Dimension Style** window.

THE BASELINE DIMENSION COMMAND allows you to calculate the distance between a series of objects and a point or baseline quickly and easily. The baseline dimension is always based on linear, angular dimensions or preexisting coordinates and is created from a baseline specified by the user. This type of dimension is primarily used to carry out multiple dimensions linked to the same line or object.

1. In this exercise you will learn how to apply dimensions with the **Baseline** command. To begin, see what the default distance used by the program is between dimensions. Open the **Annotation** tool group and click on the **Dimension style** icon.

2. In the **Dimension Style Manager** window, click on the **Modify** button and, in the **Modify Dimension Style** window, enable the Lines tab.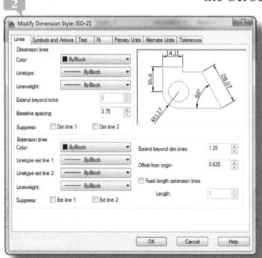

3. You can find the default baseline interval in the **Dimension lines** section; as you can see, the spacing between dimension lines in this type of dimension is 3.75. Keep this value. Once you have checked it, slightly increase the text size of the dimensions to be able to work on this exercise more comfortably. Select the Text tab.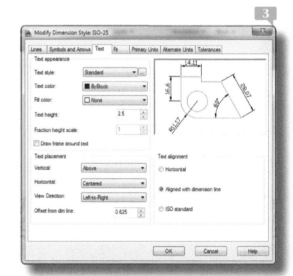

4. Double-click on the **Text height** field, enter **4** and click on the **OK** button.

The **ISO-25** dimension style is based on the Standard Text Style used by default in AutoCAD.

077

5. Close the **Dimension Style Manager** window by clicking on the **Close** button.

6. Select the **Presentation2** tab 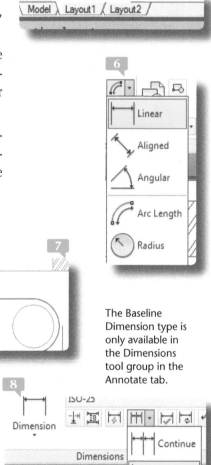 and apply a **Zoom W**indow to the shapes that make up the stove and the sink.

7. Your goal is to create a dimension from one end of the sink to the first circle and another up to the opposite side. Select the drop-down menu from the first icon in the **Annotation** tool group and choose the **Linear** option.

8. Click on the center of the vertical line on the left of the stove to select it as the origin of the first reference line and click on the left side of the first circle for the dimension text to appear automatically.

9. In order to set the dimension text, click on the same point.

10. Select the **Annotate** tab in the **Options Ribbon**, click on the arrow button in the fourth command in the **Dimensions** group, the **Continue** command, and choose the **Baseline** option.

11. You now need to specify an origin for the second reference line, as the program assumes that the baseline is the first reference line in the linear dimension you just created. Click near the center of the vertical line on the right side of the stove.

12. A first baseline dimension that goes from the linear dimension to the specified point appears. Leave the Baseline Dimension creation mode by pressing the **Escape** key and save your changes by pressing the **Ctrl + S** shortcut.

The Baseline Dimension type is only available in the Dimensions tool group in the Annotate tab.

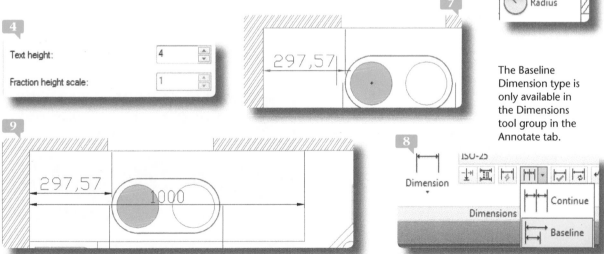

167

Applying Quick Dimensions

IMPORTANT

To delete a dimension, simply select it and press the **Delete** key or enter **erase + Enter** in the Command Line.

QUICK DIMENSIONS ALLOW you to calculate linear, radius, or diameter dimensions quickly from a multiple selection. Unlike other dimensions, the Quick Dimension command is only available in the Dimensions group in the Annotate tab.

1. In this exercise you will work with Quick Dimensions, which allow you to quickly calculate the distance between various objects. To practice you will use a sample file called **Bottles. dwg**, which you can find in the download section on our website. Copy this file to your Documents folder and open it in AutoCAD. This drawing represents a series of identical objects lined up, which you will use to see how quick dimensions are applied. Begin by zooming on the three bottles in the second row. To do this, open the **Zoom** command in the **Navigation Bar** and choose the **Zoom Window** option.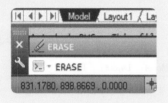

2. Draw a window that contains the three objects.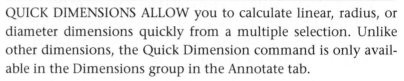

3. You can now begin the process of creating quick dimensions. The first thing to do is to increase the dimension text size so it will be visible on the drawing. To do this, click on the dialog button in the **Dimensions** tool group, in the **Annotate** tab in the **Options Ribbon**.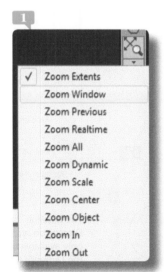

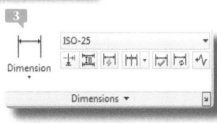

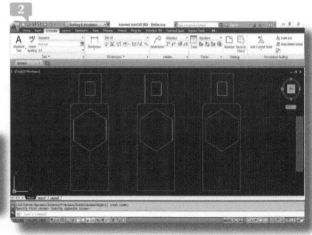

168

078

4. This opens the **Dimension Style Manager**. Select the ISO-25 style and click on the **Modify** button.

5. Go to the **Text** tab in the **Modify Dimension Style** dialog box, enter **10** in the **Text height** field, and click on the **OK** button to apply the change.

6. Leave the **Dimension Style Manager** by clicking on the **Close** button.

7. Once you have made the text height modification, click on the **Quick Dimension** icon, which is represented by a line with arrows on each end and a yellow lightning bolt, in the **Dimension** tool group in the **Annotate** tab.

8. Your goal is to create a dimension between the first bottle and the second and between the second and the third. To do this, click on the lower right corner of the first bottle and do the same on the same corners of the second and third, pressing the **Return** key after having selected the third.

9. For the dimensions to appear, enter **1743,826** in the Command Line and press the **Return** key.

10. Notice how the program has generated a series of dimensions, calculating the distance between the three selected objects. Press the X button in the current drawing and, in the emerging dialog box, press the **Yes** button.

Quick Dimensions are created from the **Model** space, not the **Paper** space.

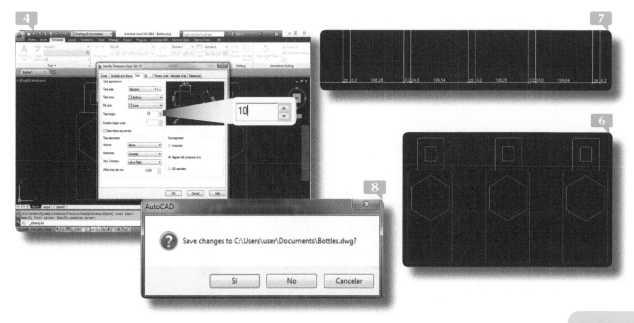

Inserting continuous dimensions

THE CONTINUE DIMENSION COMMAND allows you to line up adjacent dimensions; continuous dimensions can therefore be defined as a series of linked dimensions. Continuous dimensions are similar to baseline dimensions, the difference being that the latter take two reference points whereas the former use the last point of the last applied dimension as their first point of reference and only require you to specify the final or destination point.

1. In this exercise you will learn about the usefulness of the **Continue Dimension** command. To do this, you will continue practicing with the example drawing, updated under the name **First drawing8.dwg**, available in the download section of our website. The **Continue Dimension** command allows you to create different dimensions based on previously created dimensions. It is generally based on the most recent one and appears as an extension of it, but if you have not created any dimensions in the current session, the program will request that you create a linear, ordinate, or angular dimension to be used as the basis for the continued dimension. To begin, go to the **Model** tab by clicking on it.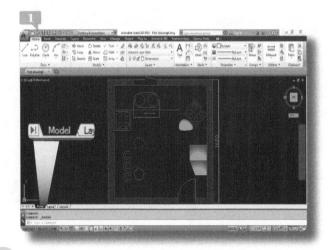

2. Open the **Zoom** command in the **Navigation Bar** and choose the **Zoom Window** option from the drop-down list.

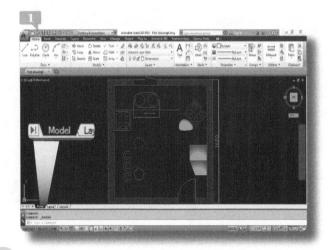
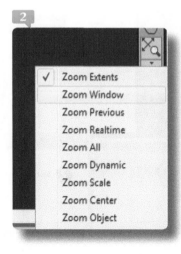

079

3. Draw a selection box over the three chairs left of the table.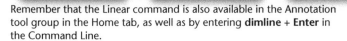

4. Begin by creating a linear dimension between the upper and middle chairs, which will be used as a reference to create the continuous dimension. Select the drop-down menu from the **Dimension** command in the **Dimensions** tool in the **Annotate** tab in the **Options Ribbon**, and click on the **Linear** command.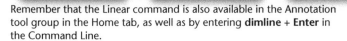

5. Click on the edge of the lower arm of the first chair, click on the edge of the upper arm of the second chair, and click on that same point to include the dimension text there.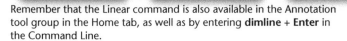

6. Once you have drawn the linear dimension, select the **Continue Dimension** dimension. Click on the **Continue** command in the **Dimensions** tool group.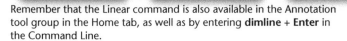

7. Since you have just created a linear dimension, the program sets it as its first point of reference for the new dimension. Once this first point has been set, include a second point. To do this, click on the edge of the lower arm of the second chair.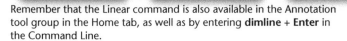

8. As you can see, the new dimension appears, displaying the distance between the selected points. You can keep on inserting points to obtain more continuous dimensions. To leave the **Continue Dimension** creation mode, press the **Return** key twice.

You can also enable **Continue Dimension** using **dimcont + Return** in the Command Line. Keep in mind that this tool is not available in the Annotation tool group in the Home tab.

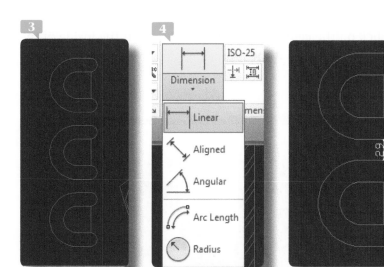

Remember that the Linear command is also available in the Annotation tool group in the Home tab, as well as by entering **dimline + Enter** in the Command Line.

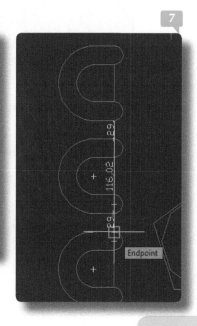

Inserting rotated dimensions

IMPORTANT

Before including a **rotated** dimension, you should calculate the inclined angle of the item to which you will apply the dimension by using the Angular Dimension tool.

ROTATED DIMENSIONS ALLOW you to apply a dimension with a specific angle before setting the first reference point and the endpoint for the dimension. The result is a dimension that, unlike aligned dimensions, can adopt a position that is not necessarily parallel, either vertically or horizontally. Now, rotated dimensions allow you to calculate the distance between rotated items.

1. In this exercise you will apply a rotated dimension, in which the dimension line is located at an angle relative to the origins of the reference line. Dimension one of the inner lines that make up the new semicircular window in the **Firstdrawing9. dwg** file, which is available for download on our website. Zoom in on the window. Open the **Zoom** command in the **Navigation Bar** and choose the **Zoom Window** option.

2. Drag a selection box containing the semicircular window on the left of the plan.

3. Calculate the degree of inclination of one of the lines that simulate the separation between the glass panes in the window by using the **Angular Dimension** tool. Open the **Dimension** command in the **Dimensions** tool group and choose the **Angular** option.

4. Click on the center of the first tilted line on the inside of the window, starting at the top.

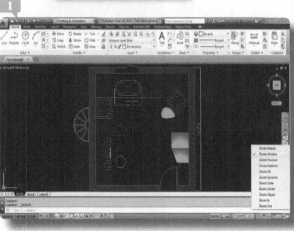

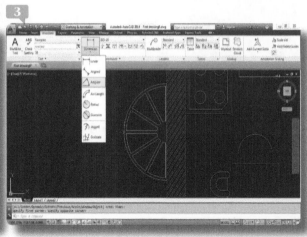

080

5. Select the second reference line by clicking on the vertical line opposite the first one.

6. You need to locate the arc for the dimension line. Type the coordinates **1944,1487** in the Command Line and press **Return.**

7. Now that the angle of inclination, 30 degrees, has been measured, create a rotated linear dimension that indicates the length of this line. Activate the **Linear Dimension** tool from the Command Line. By entering **dimlinear** and press the **Return** key.

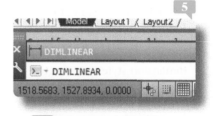

8. Press **Return** to select the object of the command and click on the part of the figure that you want.

9. Click on the center of the tilted line whose angle you recently measured to select it.

10. The dimension text automatically appears, displaying the length of the line. You need To select the **Rotate** parameter in order to rotate this dimension so that it has the same angle as the line. Type **r** in the Command Line and press **Return.**

11. The program now prompts you to specify the angle of inclination you want to apply to the linear dimension. Enter **30** and press **Return.**

12. The dimension is inclined as per your specifications. You now want to place it on the drawing. Type **1943,1362** in the Command Line and press the **Return** key.

13. To finish this exercise in which you practiced with the **Rotated Dimension** annotation tool, apply an **Extents** zoom to the drawing and save your changes using the **Ctrl + S** shortcut.

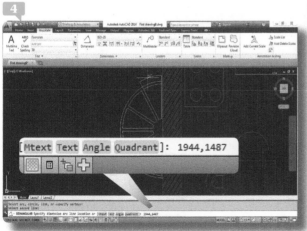

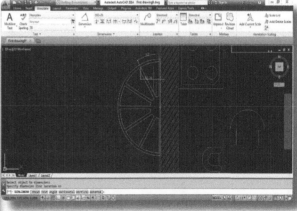

Enabling the parameters of the current command can be done by typing the capitalized letter in the Command Line.

Creating a dimension style

UP TO NOW, ALL THE DIMENSIONS you created were based on the ISO-25 style, which AutoCAD uses by default. However, you may encounter a situation where the characteristics of this style are not appropriate for the kind of work you are doing. This is why AutoCAD allows you to create new dimension styles or to modify existing styles.

1. In the following exercise you will learn how to create a new dimension style. To begin, click on the dialog box indicator in the **Dimensions** tool group.

2. The list of existing dimension styles is displayed in the **Style Manager** window. Click on the **New** button.

3. Type **Test** in the **New Style Name** field of the **Create New Dimension Style** window.

4. Base the new style on the original, unmodified **ISO-25** style. Therefore, keep this style selected in the **Start With** field and click on the **Continue** button.

5. The **Create Dimension Style**: test window consist of seven tabs in which you can change the main features of the standard style in order to create a new one. Set a dimension line color and change its width. Click on the arrow button in the **Color** field and select **Magenta**.

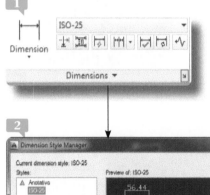

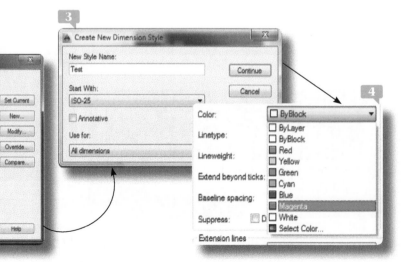

6. Click on the arrow button in the **Lineweight** field and choose the **0.40 mm** option, for instance.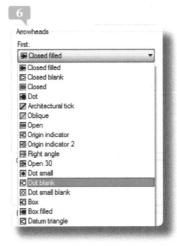

7. Click on the **Symbols and Arrows** tab.

8. Make the ends of the dimension display as white dots instead of filled arrows. Click on the arrow button in the **First** field, in the **Arrowheads** section, and choose the **Dot blank** option.

9. Select the **Text** tab.

10. The Text tab allows you to change the text options for a dimension. Open the drop-down menu in the Vertical field, in the **Text Placement** section, and click on the **Centered** option.

11. Click on the **Alternate units** tab and check the **Display alternate units** option to display two units in your drawing.

12. Open the **Unit format** field and click on the **Architectural** option.

13. Click on the **OK** button to create the new dimension style, and, after seeing that the new style already appears in the style list and that it is selected, click on the **Close** button in the **Dimension Style Manager**.

Notice that the new style, called **Test**, appears selected in the Style field of the Dimensions tool group. This means that, unless you specify otherwise, any further dimensions will be created with this style.

IMPORTANT

The Adjust tab in the Dimension Style Manager allows you to control the general scale for the dimension style and the location of the text based on the type of dimension and its position in the drawing. It is possible to define the units the dimensions will use in their text in the **Main units** tab. The **Tolerances** tab allows you to control how they are viewed and the format for the dimension text tolerances.

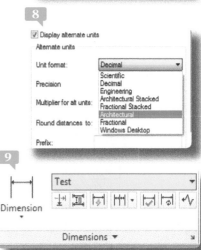

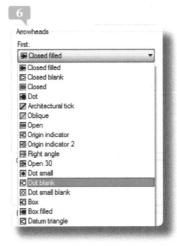

Flipping dimension arrows

IN AUTOCAD 2014, the grips at the ends of a dimension include the Flip Arrow option that allows you to change the direction of any of the two arrows on the dimension line. As in earlier versions of the program, this option is also included in the Dimension Line pop-up menu.

1. In this exercise you will learn how to flip the arrows in a dimension, specifically in the linear dimension that shows the length of the counter that contains the sink in the **First drawing9.dwg** example file. To do this, go to the **Presentation2** tab and click on the dimension to select it.

2. Place the cursor on the grip on the left of the dimension line and select the **Flip Arrow** option from the menu.

3. Notice how the upper arrow automatically changes its direction. Dimension grips also allow you to change the position of the text in the dimension. Repeat the process to flip the arrow on the right in the same dimension. Place the cursor on the grip on the right end of the dimension and click on the **Flip Arrow** option.

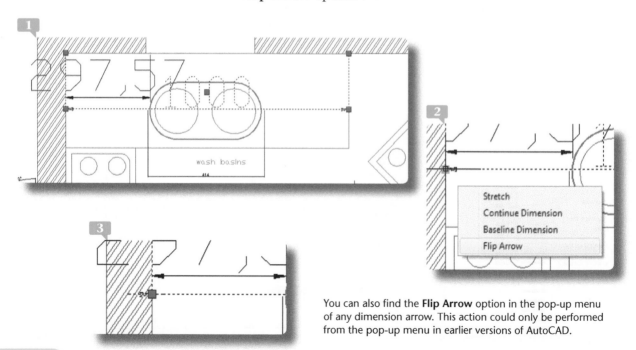

You can also find the **Flip Arrow** option in the pop-up menu of any dimension arrow. This action could only be performed from the pop-up menu in earlier versions of AutoCAD.

082

4. Notice how the direction of that arrow in the dimension also changes.

5. Before finishing this exercise, see how to use another command included in the **Dimensions** tool group. This command, which you have not discussed up to now, is the **Center Mark** command, with which the program automatically marks the center of circles and arcs. It is extremely simple to use. Simply activate it and select the arc or circle whose center you want to mark. Unselect the dimension by pressing the **Escape** key.

6. Click on the arrow button in the Dimensions tool group and click on the **Center Mark** option, the third one in the lower panel.

7. Click on any of the circles that represent the burners on the left of the plan.

8. As you can see, a cross appears in the exact center of the selected arc. Apply an **Extents** zoom and save your changes. Open the Zoom command in the **Navigation Bar** and choose the Zoom Extents option.

9. Click on the **Save** icon in the **Quick Access Toolbar**.

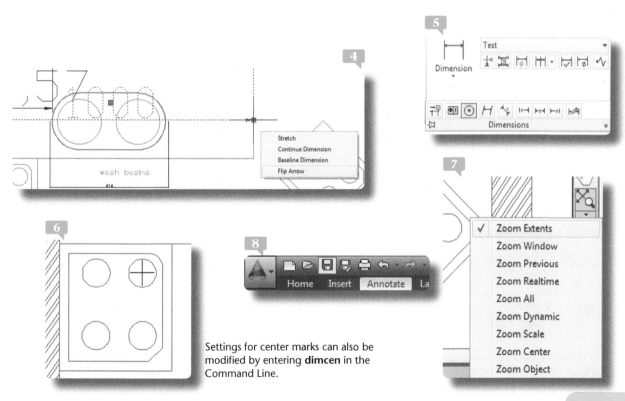

wash basins

Stretch
Continue Dimension
Baseline Dimension
Flip Arrow

Settings for center marks can also be modified by entering **dimcen** in the Command Line.

Zoom Extents
Zoom Window
Zoom Previous
Zoom Realtime
Zoom All
Zoom Dynamic
Zoom Scale
Zoom Center
Zoom Object

Annotating with the Leader command

AUTOCAD ALLOWS YOU TO INCLUDE SMALL ANNOTATIONS in drawings using the Quick Leader command. Leaders can be a very important part of a plan as they often provide necessary information such as object materials and chronological and situational references for each item in the drawing.

IMPORTANT

Unlike dimensions, leaders only display one arrow head on one end. Now, leaders are lines or splines with a dimension end and a Multiline Text object on the other. In some cases, a small horizontal line, called a **connection line**, connects the text to the leader line.

1. In the following exercise you will learn how to include comments in a drawing. Enter **Lead** in the Command Line and choose the **QLEADER** command from the Autocomplete menu.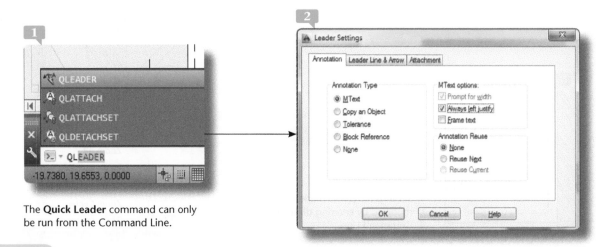

2. Before specifying the points in the leader you will add to the drawing, open the **Leader Settings** window to see its default settings. Press the **Return** key.

3. This opens the **Leader Settings** window, which, as you can see, contains three tabs. The Annotation tab allows you to set the type of annotation for the leader, set multiple text options, and indicate if you want to reuse the annotation. Click on the checkbox for the **Always left justify** option in the **MText options** section.

4. The program will now align the text on the left and prompt you for its width. Click on the **Leader Line & Arrow** tab.

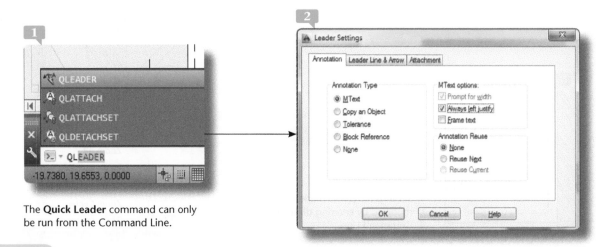

The **Quick Leader** command can only be run from the Command Line.

178

5. In the **Leader & Arrow** tab you can specify whether the leader line will be straight or a spline, set the format for the end of the dimension, specify the number of points it can be made up of, and set angle limitations. Click on the arrow button in the selected option in the **Arrowhead** section and click on the **Closed blank** option in the pop-up menu.

6. Click on the **OK** button to leave the settings window while applying the changes you have made.

7. You must now specify the first point in the leader, that is, the final point of the arrow. Type the coordinates **179,81** in the Command Line and press **Return**.

8. Set the next point, whose end will contain the text, by entering the coordinates **210,70**, press **Return**, and press the **Return** key again to leave the point setting mode.

9. The program prompts you to type the first line of text. Type **Gradient** and press the **Return** key twice.

10. Once you have added the leader at the selected points, you can modify its contents or format by using the Text Editor. Double-click on the leader text to select it.

11. This opens the **Text Editor** tab in the Options Ribbon, with which you have worked earlier. Change any of the available settings in the tool groups, press the **Close text editor** button, and save your changes.

IMPORTANT

When the **Mtext** option is active in the **Annotation** tab in the leader settings window, the **Link** tab will be active and will allows you to set the location of the link between the leader lines and the Multiline Text annotation.

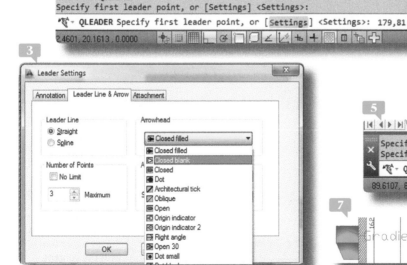

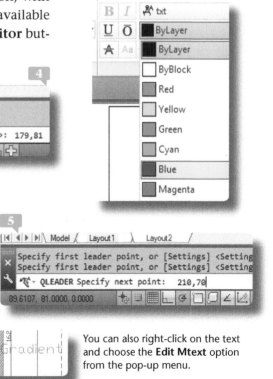

You can also right-click on the text and choose the **Edit Mtext** option from the pop-up menu.

Applying Multileaders

AUTOCAD 2014 ALLOWS YOU TO automatically create Multileaders and to change the orientation of leader lines with the notes. You can now place a leader object at the end of a leader dimension, the leader's connection segment, or the first content.

1. Begin this exercise by applying a zoom to the chairs on the example plan. Click on the **Multileader** command in the **Annotate** tab.

2. Draw the leader with the default drawing option, which implies that the first point you need to select is the end of the leader, where the arrow is displayed. Click on the approximate center of the seat of the lower chair to put the end of the leader line there.

3. Specify the location of the connection segment of the leader. Type the coordinates **57,48** in the Command Line and press the **Return** key.

4. A text box now appears next to the connection segment to type in the contents, and the Text Editor tab appears to allow you to modify the text. In this case, type **Seat** and click on the **Close** button of the Text Editor.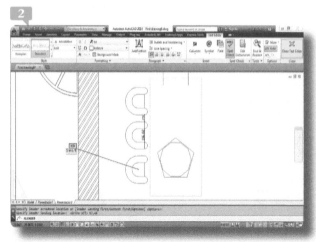

5. Practice with the Connection segment first and the Content first options. Click on the **Multileader** command in the **Lead-**

An advantage of **multileaders** is that they can be organized in several ways to give more order and coherence to a drawing.

By default, the dimension side will be drawn first due to the leader type. If you want to change this option, begin by selecting the leader connection segment, that is, the end with the arrow, or start with the content.

084

ers group again, type **l** and press the **Return** key to draw a line beginning at the connection end.

6. You can now draw the multileader. Type the coordinates **97,31** in the Command Line and press the **Return** key.

7. Notice how the opposite end of the leader line, where the text will be located, appears on screen. For the dimension end, type the coordinates **86,35** in the Command Line and press the **Return** key.

8. Type **Right armrest** and press the **Close Text Editor** command.

9. Draw a third leader with the Content First option, which will be added to the left armrest. Enable the **Multileader** command again, type **C** in the Command Line and press the **Return** key.

10. The letters **abc** appear next to the cursor. It is necessary to set the space that the leader text will take up. Type the coordinates **97,34** in the Command Line, press **Return**, type in the coordinates **100,37** and press **Return**.

11. Type **Left armrest** and click on the **Close Text Editor** command.

12. You can now draw the multileader at the selected point. Enter the coordinates **76,55** in the Command Line and press **Return**.

13. To finish the exercise, apply an **Extents** zoom to the plan and save your changes by using the **Ctrl + S** shortcut.

IMPORTANT

The **Collect** command allows you to compile and associate several Multileaders that contain blocks into a single group and to link them to a single leader line, vertically, horizontally, or in a specific area, depending on the drawing.

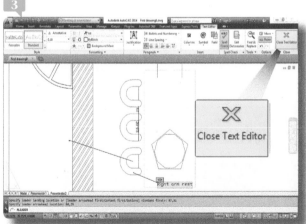

AutoCAD 2014 contains new multifunctional grips for greater and better control of Multileaders.

You can also leave the Text Editor by pressing the **Escape** key.

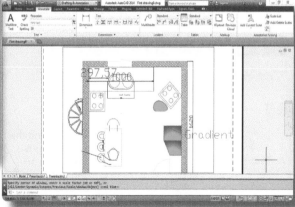

Setting annotation scale

ANNOTATION SCALE is simply another object property that can be applied to Multiline Texts, blocks, and attributes, that is, objects that are normally used to annotate drawings. These become annotative objects when the annotative property is enabled. When creating an annotative object, the current annotative scale will be applied automatically and objects will be drawn or viewed with the correct size on paper.

1. Annotative scale can only be set from the **Model** space; enable it by clicking on its tab.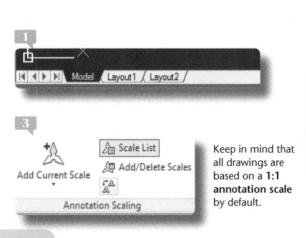

2. Notice now that only the dimensions created in the model space appear here; this demonstrates the advantage of using presentations or paper space to avoid cluttering your work. Click on the **Annotation Scale** command in the **Status Bar**, which is **1:1**, and select **1:2**.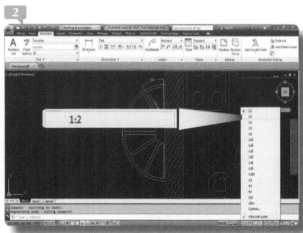

3. The scale list can be customized if you choose the Custom option in the menu or you click on the Scale list command in the Annotation scaling tool group, which is only included in the **Annotate** tab. Click on this command, which is the first icon in the vertical list.

4. The **Edit Drawing Scales** window allows you to customize the list. You can, for instance, delete scales you are not going

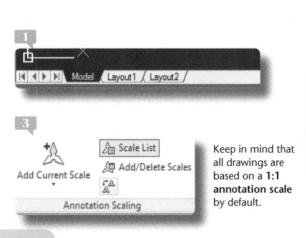

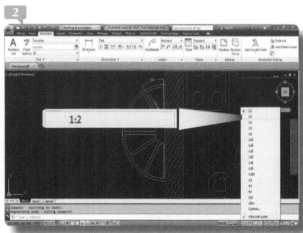

Keep in mind that all drawings are based on a **1:1 annotation scale** by default.

to use (such as the ones in inches), change the order of the scales, or edit existing scales. Click on the **Cancel** button.

5. Once you have set the annotation scale, you only need to select activate the **Annotative** property in the objects you want to change to that type. You can do this via annotative styles. For instance, when creating a multileader, you can simply open the **Modify Multileader Style** window and make sure that the **Annotative** check box in the Scale section of the **Leader Structure** tab is checked. You can also modify existing objects to make them annotative. Go back to the **Presentation2** tab and apply an **Extents** zoom to the plan.

6. Double-click on the **Seat** multileader in the drawing so that the Properties panel appears. (Make sure you click on the leader and not the text.)

7. The option you are looking for is in the **Various** section of this panel. Click on the **Annotative** field and, in the field on the right, choose the **Yes** option.

8. Close the Properties panel by clicking on the X button in its **Title Bar** and unselect the leader by pressing **Escape**.

9. Place the cursor on the multileader you just modified and notice that a special symbol, which corresponds to the **Annotative** property, appears.

10. Return to the **Model** space by clicking on its tab and finish this exercise by returning the drawing to its usual, **1:1** scale from the **Status Bar**.

IMPORTANT

The dialog boxes with which text objects, dimensions, and multileaders are defined contain the **Annotative** check mark. Checking it makes the object in question annotative.

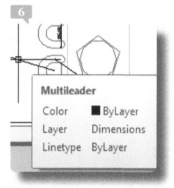

You can delete all the changes you have made and restore the default scale list by clicking on the **Restore** button in the **Edit Drawing Scales** window

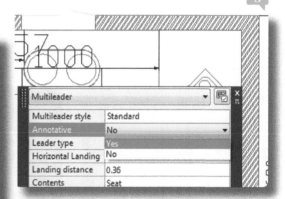

Normally, annotative objects are defined on a paper size. The size of annotative objects in the Presentation and Model spaces are determined by the annotation scale set for them.

Utilities: Measurements and surfaces

IMPORTANT

Another command found within the **Utilities** tool is the **Quick calculator**. Clicking on the arrowhead in **Utilities** will lead you to **ID Point**, which gives you the exact coordinates of any point on the screen, and **Point Style** which is, used to control the format of all the points you want to draw.

AFTER DEALING WITH THE LIMIT SECTION, it is very useful to address the issue of how to check measures without having to limit them and learning how to calculate surfaces is essential.

1. For this exercise, continue working with **Firstdrawing.dwg**. Go to the **Utilities** tool group, in the **Home** tab.

2. Click on the **Measure** icon's arrowhead to see the options that it offers. In the drop-down menu are all the measurement commands. To see an example click on **Distance**. Click on the right lower point and the upper right point of the counter to find its width, which appears in the Command Line. Press **Escape** to exit the command.

3. Follow the same steps of the previous section to practice with the **Radius** and **Angle** commands.

4. Select **Area** and click on the four inside corners of the room in the right order until it is fully colored in green, press **Return** to measure the selected area and perimeter, which appear in the Command Line. Press Escape to exit the command.

5. Practice with the **Area** command on polylines. Draw a rectangle that defines the whole area of the room. Click on

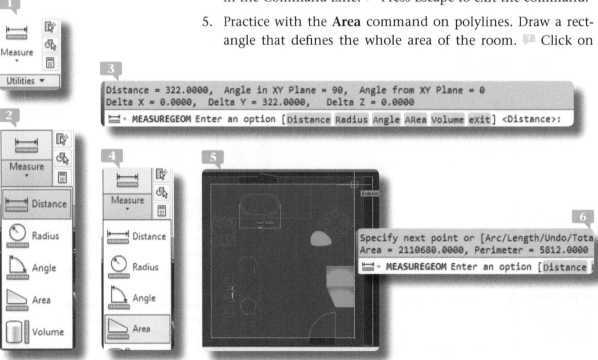

184

086

Area, type **O** (for Object) and click on **Return** to select the polyline that has been drawn, This will measure the selected area (colored in green) and perimeter, which appear in the Command Line.

6. Keeping this order selected, type **R** for **Area**, then **A** for **Add** and finally **O** for **Object** to add different surfaces from polylines. Select the two circular sinks in the counter, which are now colored in green, to find the sum of both areas, which can be found in the Command Line.

7. Click on **Return** and type **S** for **Subtract** and **O** for **Object** in order to subtract the previous sum of surfaces based on polylines. Select the outline of the sink on the right, which is now colored in red, to be subtracted from the whole so that only the area of the sink on the left can be found in the Command Line.

8. The **Volume** command is the same as the **Area** command, except that height is required for **Area**.

9. By clicking on the first of the icons to the right of the **Utilities** tool group, within the **Home** tab corresponding to **Quick select**, you can select objects by their color, layer, line type, etc. The second icon in the **Utilities** tool group selects all objects in the drawing.

7

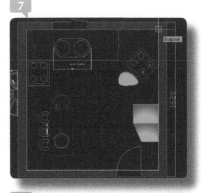

8

```
:e/Radius/Angle/ARea/Volume] <Distance>: _area
  first corner point or [Object Add area Subtract area eXit] <Object>: o
```

9

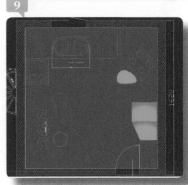

10

```
.51
80.0000, Perimeter = 5812.0000
GEOM Enter an option [Distance Radius Angle ARea Volume eXit] <ARea>: ar
```

11   **12**

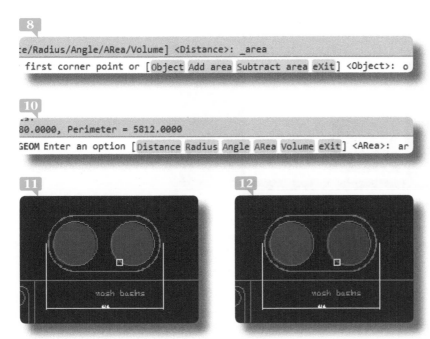

13

Inserting tables

A TABLE IS AN OBJECT THAT CONTAINS information arranged in rows and columns. You can create a table object based on a table or a blank Table Style, In additon to by linking a table to the data in a Microsoft Excel spreadsheet. After inserting it in an AutoCAD file, a table can be modified in many ways with its grips or its Properties panel.

1. In this exercise you will learn how to insert a simple table with the standard default style in the **First drawing9.dwg** example file. To begin, click on the **Table** button in the **Tables** tool in the **Annotate** tab.

2. This opens the **Insert Table** window, from which you can see all the table's default characteristics. Notice that the selected Table Style is the **Standard** style. You can insert a blank table or import data from an outside source or from the drawing itself. Keep the **Start from empty table** option selected in the **Insert options** section.

3. In the **Insert options** section you can choose to either specify an insertion point by typing the location of the table's upper

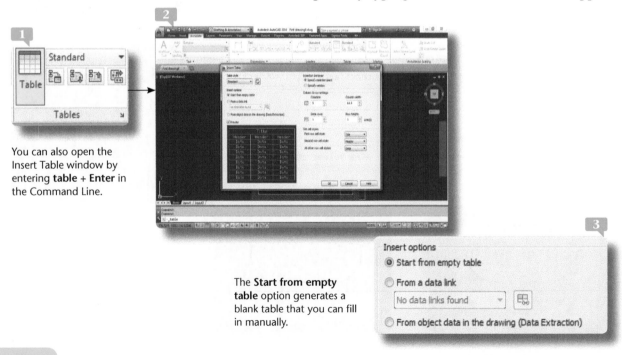

You can also open the Insert Table window by entering **table + Enter** in the Command Line.

The **Start from empty table** option generates a blank table that you can fill in manually.

Insert options
- ⦿ Start from empty table
- ○ From a data link
  - No data links found
- ○ From object data in the drawing (Data Extraction)

left corner or to specify the window by typing a size and a location for it. Keep the **Specify insertion point** option in the **Insertion behavior** section.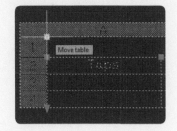

4. You can specify the number of columns, their width, the number of rows and their height in the **Column & row settings** section. Double-click on the **Data rows** field and enter **2**.

5. Keep the default cell styles in the **Define cell styles** section and click on the **OK** button to insert the table.

6. The Command Line now requests the insertion point for the table. Type the coordinates **1247,1249** and press the **Return** key.

7. When inserting the table, the **Text Editor** tab is enabled automatically and the first cell is displayed in Edit mode in the graphic area so you can type in it. Enter **Components** and press the **Return** key.

8. This takes you to the next cell in the table, which is also displayed in Edit mode. Enter **Taps** and press **Return**.

9. Click on the **Close Text Editor** button in the **Text Editor** tab.

10. To check how the table looks, apply a **Zoom W**indow to it.

11. To finish the exercise, save your changes by clicking on the Save icon in the **Quick Access Toolbar**.

087

IMPORTANT

The multifunctional grips that appear when you select a table allow you to modify it in many ways; for instance, you can stretch the height of a table in a uniform manner, change the width of the columns, move the entire table, etc.

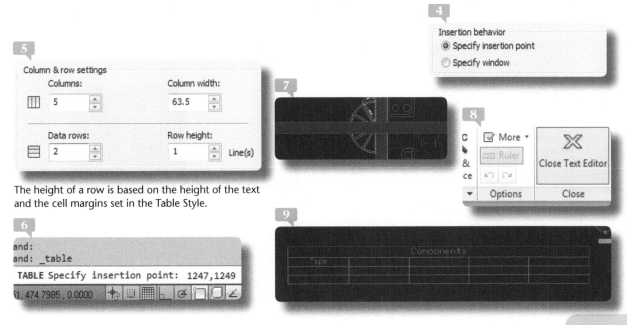

Insertion behavior
◉ Specify insertion point
◯ Specify window

Column & row settings

Columns:	Column width:
5	63.5

Data rows:	Row height:
2	1 Line(s)

The height of a row is based on the height of the text and the cell margins set in the Table Style.

More ▾
Ruler

Close Text Editor

Options   Close

and:
and: _table
TABLE Specify insertion point: 1247,1249
1, 474.7985 , 0.0000

Creating Table Styles

IMPORTANT

To create a new Table Style from an existing table, select it, open its pop-up menu, click on the Table Style option, and, in the submenu that contains this option, click on the **Save as New Table Style** option.

Save as New Table Style...
Set As Table in Current Table Style

Standard
✓ Test

AUTOCAD ALLOWS YOU TO CREATE AND MODIFY Table Styles. The Standard style is composed by merged cells with centered text. This cell style, called **Title**, can be used to create a new rank in a table's title. One way of creating a new table style is by selecting a table that already exists in the drawing and modify it as needed.

1. In this exercise you will define a new table style with different cell styles. To begin, insert another table in the drawing. Click on the **Table** command in the **Tables** tool group.

2. You can modify both the Table Style and the cell style from the **Insert Table** window. Click on the **Data row** field and type 3.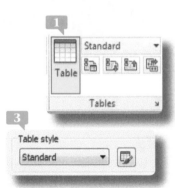

3. Click on the icon next to the **Table Style** field.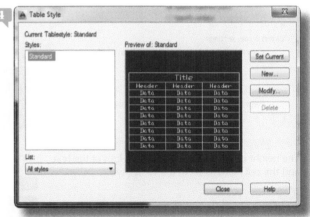

4. You can create a new Table Style, modify or delete existing style, or define a selected style in the Styles list from the **Table Style** window. In this case, click on the **New** button.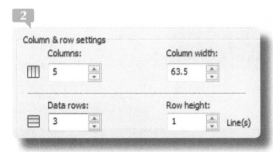

5. Type **Test** in the **Create New Table** style window and click **Continue**.

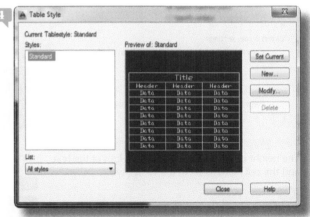

You can also set all the **style variables** from the Command Line entering specific values.

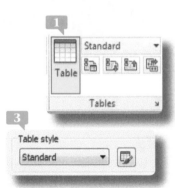

You can also apply a style to a table from its pop-up menu, selecting it from the list that appears on the lower part of the menu.

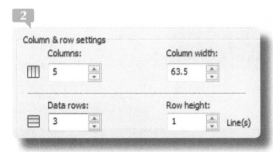

You can access the **Table Style** dialog window both from the Tables tool group in the Annotate tab In additon to from the appropriate command in the Annotation tool group in the Home tab of the Options Ribbon.

088

6. This opens the **New Table Style** window. You can modify existing cell styles or create new ones in the Cell Styles section by clicking on the black arrow button next to the data list or on the icon next to it. Open the **Fill color** field and choose **Green**.

7. The **Alignment** field defines the alignment of the text in the table cell. Open it and choose the **Middle Center** option.

8. Select the **Text** tab to view the text properties.

9. In this section you can modify the Text Style. In addition to the style, you can also change the height, angle (from -359 to +359 degrees), and text color. Open the **Text color** field and choose **Blue** from the list.

10. The last tab, **Borders**, allows you to set the look of the grid lines in the current cell style. Select it, click on the Lineweight field, and choose **0.35 mm**.

11. Open the **Color** field and choose **Magenta**.

12. Click on the first icon in the **Spacing** section, **All borders**, and click **OK** to create the new Table Style.

13. Click on the **Close** button in the **Table Style** field and click on the **OK** button in the **Insert Table** window.

14. Click on any point in your drawing to insert the table and notice that it has the characteristics you set. Finally, save your changes.

IMPORTANT

The **Select table to start from** button allows you to select a table from your drawing to which the parameters set in the Table Styles window will be applied.

Starting table
Select table to start from:

8

Spacing: | 1.125

Apply the selected properties to borders by clicking the buttons above.

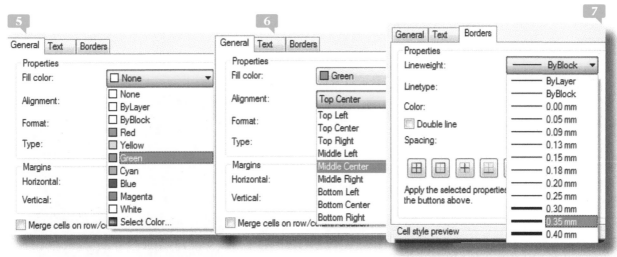

You can modify cell properties such as fill color, alignment, and content format, in additon to data or tag types, in the **General** tab.

The Table direction menu in the General section allows you to choose whether the table will be read from the top down or bottom up, which implies that the title and headings appear on the lower part of it.

Creating geometric constraints

PARAMETRIC DRAWING ALLOWS YOU TO add constraints to 2D geometry. Constraints are rules that determine the position of objects based on other objects and their dimensions. Constraints are normally used in the design phase of projects.

1. To practice using geometric constraints, use the **Restrictions. dwg** file, which you can download from our website. Once you have opened the file, enable the **Parametric** tab in the **Options Ribbon**.

2. Click on the first, small icon in the **Geometric** group, which corresponds to coincidence restriction.

3. Coincidence constraints forces two points to coincide, whatever the shape of the two objects. It forces one point to rest on any other point of a second object. Place the cursor on the upper side of the white, straight line until a red circle appears.

4. This is a coincidence point. Now, locate the cursor on the approximate center of the line and click on the new coincidence point.

5. You need to select a second object, which will rest on the line. Locate the cursor on the white circle and, after seeing that only the central coincidence point appears, click on it.

6. Based on the specified points, the two objects now coincide

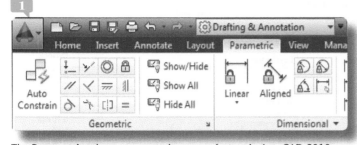

The **Parametric** tab was presented as a new feature in AutoCAD 2010.

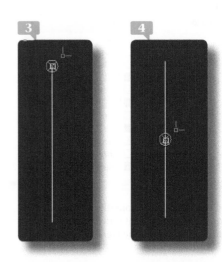

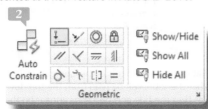

perfectly. If you place the cursor on the blue point, which indicates the existence of constraints between two objects, the Constraint type applied icon appears. [5]

7. Concentric constraints force both circles and arcs or ellipses to maintain the same center. In the **Geometric** tool group, click on the third icon, which corresponds to concentric constraints. [6]

8. Click on the white circle and then click on the red circle to select it as the second object. [7]

9. What happens if you try to change, for instance, the line's orientation? Select the vertical white line, click on the lower grip, and, holding down the mouse button, drag it upward following a 90-degree angle until the line is horizontal. Click again. [8]

10. The circle maintains the coincidence with the line, as does the concentric circle that remains inside the main circle. The parallel constraint forces the two lines to be parallel. Select the first icon in the second line of the Geometric tool group, which corresponds to parallel constraints.

11. Click on the magenta line and then on the blue line.

12. The second selected line has tilted itself to become parallel with the first. [•] There is also a perpendicular constraint, which makes one line perpendicular to the other. Click on the second icon in the second row of constraints.

13. Click on the blue line to select it as the first object, and then click on the green line and save your changes.

IMPORTANT

You can choose from a broad range of constraints, each one of which has a distinct icon: horizontal, vertical, parallel, concentric, coincidence, fixed, perpendicular, softened, etc.

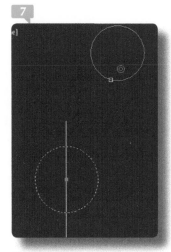

The advantage of working with **constraints** is that allow you to make changes that affect all of the restricted objects.

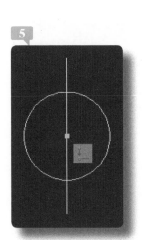

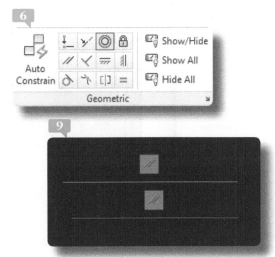

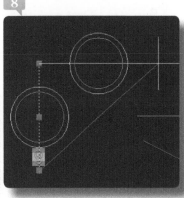

Applying automatic constraints

IN AUTOCAD 2010 AND LATER VERSIONS you can apply geometric constraints automatically to selected objects or to all objects in a drawing that fulfill certain constraint conditions.

1. In this exercise you will learn how to apply automatic constraints to a series of objects. Before you begin, delete the constraints applied in the previous exercise on several objects. Click on the **Delete Constraints** command in the **Manage** tool group.

2. You must now select the objects from which you want to remove the constraints. In this case, click on the magenta, blue, and green lines and press the **Return** key to confirm the selection and remove the applied constraints.

3. Once you are done deleting the constraints, look at the Settings window for automatic constraints. To do this, click on the bottom right arrow button in the Geometric tool group.

4. This opens the **Constraint Settings** dialog box, which contains three tabs: **Geometric**, which is active by default, **Dimensional, and AutoConstrain.** Click on the third tab to display its contents.

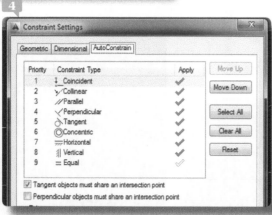

When **deleting constraints**, the objects involved do not return to their original positions; rather, the constraint applied to them simply disappears.

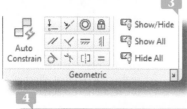

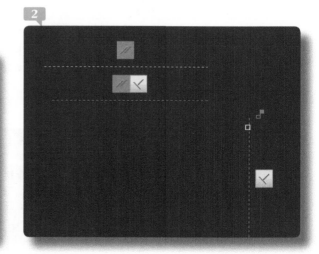

090

5. Keep all the values as they are and proceed. Click on the **OK** button.

6. Let's apply automatic constraints to two of the three color lines. To do this, click on the **Auto constraints** button in the **Geometric** tool group.

7. Select the objects to which the program will apply the constraints. As you pointed out earlier, click on the magenta line, and then click on the green line and press **Return** to apply the automatic constraints.

8. Depending on the position of the two selected lines, the program applies up to two constraints, as you can see on the icons that indicate it: a horizontal and a perpendicular one. Apply other constraints, this time on the two parallel lines. To do this, click on the **Auto constrain** command.

9. Click on the magenta and blue lines, in this order, and press **Return** to apply the automatic constraints.

10. As you can see, the parallel constraints are applied. You can use automatic constraints in those cases in which objects are placed perfectly and you need to restrict them. To finish this exercise, save your changes by clicking on the **Save** icon in the **Quick Access Toolbar**.

IMPORTANT

By default, constraints applied to selected objects are the ones displayed in the **Auto constrain** tab of the **Constraint Settings** window and in the default order. If you are interested, you can change this order by selecting the constraint type and clicking on the **Raise or Lower** buttons on the right. If you wish, you can disable constraints from this list so that they are not applied automatically.

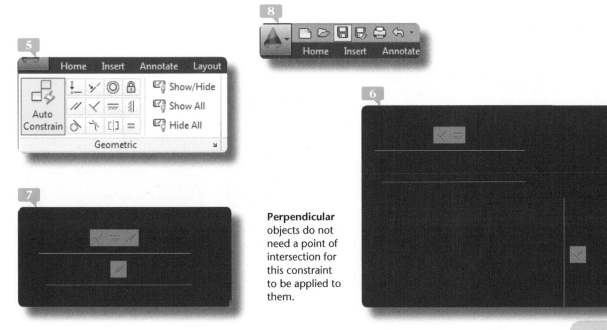

Perpendicular objects do not need a point of intersection for this constraint to be applied to them.

Creating dimensional constraints

DIMENSIONAL CONSTRAINTS DETERMINE the distances or angles between objects or points of objects and the size of the objects. Constraints of this type include a number and a value, and it is possible to apply them between two points, selecting one or a pair of objects.

1. In this exercise you will learn how to apply dimensional constraints. Begin by applying a linear constraint to the line that forms a tangent over the circles. To do this, click on the **Linear** command in the **Dimensional** tool group.

2. Specify the first constraint point. You need to restrict the two ends of the selected line; therefore, place the cursor on the left end of the straight white line and, once the red circle appears, click on it.

3. Move the cursor over the opposite end of the line and, when the red circle appears, click to set the second constraint point.

4. Specify the location of the dimension line. type the coordinates **118,209** in the Command Line, press **Return** twice to include the dimensional constraint, and leave the Edit mode for the constraint you inserted.

By default, dimensional constraints are **dynamic** and therefore perfect for parametric drawing for normal or design purposes.

Linear Aligned Show/Hide Show All Hide All

Dimensional ▾

If you modify the value of a dimensional constraint, the program makes an assessment of all the constraints on the objects and automatically updates the affected objects.

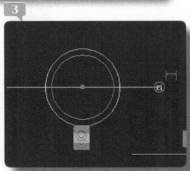

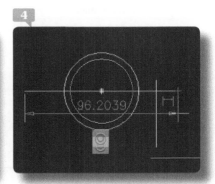

091

5. Apply a diametric constraint that restricts the diameter of the red circle. Click on the **Diameter** command, the second in the group of four located in the center of the **Dimensional** tool group. 5

6. Select the arc or circle to be constrained. In this case, click on the red circle. 6

7. Once again, specify the point where the dimension line will be. Type the coordinates **94,171** in the Command Line and press **Return**. 7

8. The diametric dimension constraint is inserted at the specified point, ready to be edited. Press the **Enter** key to leave the Edit mode and see the results.

9. Apply an angular dimension constraint. To do this, click on the third icon in the group of four in the **Dimensional** tool group. 8

10. Select the first and second line or arc. In this case, click on the magenta line and, as the second line, click on the green line.

11. Specify the location of the dimension line. 9 In the Command Line, type the coordinates **224,122** and press **Return** twice, the first time to accept the value and the second to undo the dimension selection.

12. A selection box appears, warning you about the possibility of producing an over-constraint of the geometry if you apply the intended dimension constraint. In this case, click on the **Create a reference dimension** option. 10

IMPORTANT

An **over-constraint** occurs when you try to apply a constraint to an object that already has one, leading to an incompatibility between both.

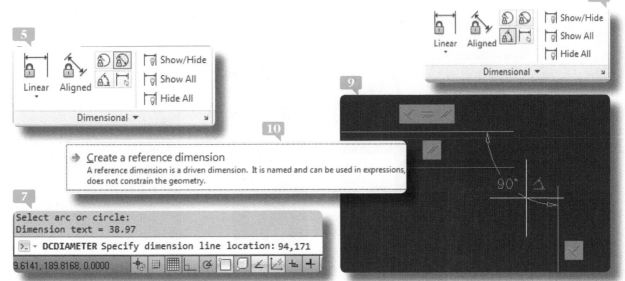

→ Create a reference dimension
A reference dimension is a driven dimension. It is named and can be used in expressions, does not constrain the geometry.

Select arc or circle:
Dimension text = 38.97

DCDIAMETER Specify dimension line location: 94,171

9.6141, 189.8168, 0.0000

Turning dynamic constraints into associative constraints

DIMENSIONAL CONSTRAINTS ARE DYNAMIC by default, and are ideal for parametric drawing for normal and design purposes, as they can be displayed or hidden according to you's needs. Dynamic constraints can be turned into annotational constraints. To do this, you must use the Constraint Settings palette.

1. In this exercise you will learn how to transform dimensional constraints, which are dynamic by default, into annotational constraints. The first thing you need to do is to select the constraint you wish to modify and open its Properties palette. Click on the linear dimension constraint you created on the white line. 🔲

2. If you have Quick Properties enabled, the panel will appear floating on the screen. However, in this case, you need to access the general Properties palette for the object. Right-click on the blue square located on the constraint and, in the pop-up menu, select the **Properties** option. 🔲

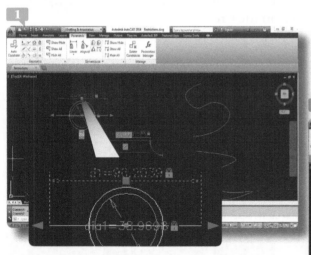

You can also access the Settings panel for an object by using the dialog box indicator in the **Properties** tool group of the Home tab.

Quick Properties for objects can be enabled with the next to last icon in the Status Bar or by using the **Ctrl + Shift + P** shortcut.

3. The field you are looking for, **Constraint Settings**, is located in the **Constraint** section of the Settings palette. In this case, change the Contraint Form to Annotational. Click on the Constraint Form, use the pop-up menu in the **Dynamic** option, and choose **Annotational**.

4. The change is immediate. Notice how the contents of the Settings palette have changed to display all the properties of the applied dimension type, which, in this case, is linear. You can change any of these properties if you like. Unlike dynamic constraints, annotational constraints are displayed using the current dimension style, their size changes when zooming, they offer complete grip functions, and they are displayed on the drawing. For now, close this palette by clicking on the X button in its **Title Bar**.

5. Press the **Escape** key to see what the annotational dimension looks like.

6. As you can see, the look of the annotational constraint differs considerably from the dynamic dimensional constraint, and it resembles conventional dimensions. To finish this exercise, save the changes by clicking on the **Save** button in the **Quick Access Toolbar**.

IMPORTANT

If you want the text for annotational constraints to be displayed in the same format as the one used for dimensions, set the CONSTRAINTNAMEFORMAT system variable to 1.

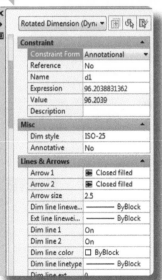

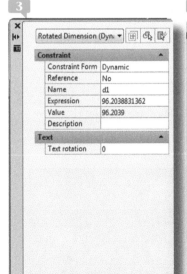

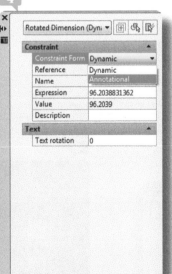

After making the drawing, you can use the Settings palette to convert annotational constraints to dynamic constraints.

Inferring constraints

THANKS TO THE INFER CONSTRAINTS FUNCTION, available from the Status Bar, the program can deduce your designs intentions while drawing or editing the geometry. Inferring constraints is used with references to objects and polar tracking, and it can only be carried out if the objects correspond to the constraint conditions.

1. In this exercise you will see how, when drawing a series of objects with inferred constraints enabled, coincidence constraints are applied to the lines that make them up. Click on the first icon in the **Status Bar**, which corresponds to the **Infer constraints** function.

2. Once **Infer Constraints** is enabled, begin by drawing a rectangle. Go to the Home tab in the **Options Ribbon** and click on the **Rectangle** icon in the **Draw** group.

3. As you know, you can draw figures directly on the work area or by typing coordinates. In this case, enter the coordinates **37,90** as the first corner point and press **Return**.

4. Enter the coordinates **130,56** as the opposite corner and press the **Return** key to obtain the rectangle.

5. Notice how the rectangle is created with, in this case, five geometric constraints: four parallel and one coincidence. This

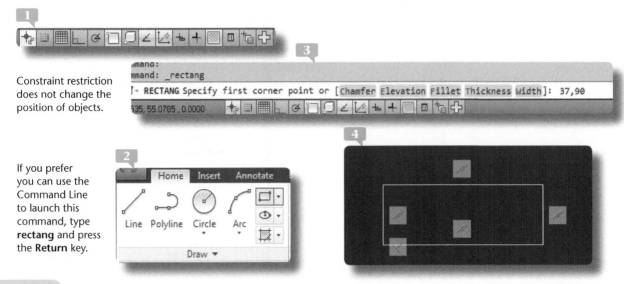

Constraint restriction does not change the position of objects.

Command: _rectang
RECTANG Specify first corner point or [Chamfer Elevation Fillet Thickness Width]: 37,90
635, 55.0785 , 0.0000

If you prefer you can use the Command Line to launch this command, type **rectang** and press the **Return** key.

Home   Insert   Annotate

Line   Polyline   Circle   Arc

Draw ▾

198

coincidence constraint is deduced from the **Close** option between the starting point of the first line segment and the final point of the last segment. Apply a modification command to the rectangle to see the type of constraint inferred by the program. Click on the **Fillet** command in the **Modify** tool group, which is displayed as a right angle and an arc. [5]

6. In the Command Line, enter **r** [6] to change the offset radius value, press **Return**, type 8 as the fillet radius [7] and press **Return** again.

7. Select the two lines in the rectangle you want to offset. Click on the upper line and on the line on the left and notice how the offset is applied. [8]

8. In addition to applying the change, two constraints are inferred from this action, in this case, tangency constraints. Let's apply the change again on the opposite corner of the rectangle. Select the **Fillet** command again, click on the lower and right lines of the rectangle and see the results. [9]

9. When moving, copying, or stretching with the Infer constraints option enabled, you can apply coincidence, perpendicular, parallel, or tangency constraints between the object you are editing and the object to which you are referring. The base point for the object must be a valid constraint point for that object. When editing the final point of a line with grips to move it horizontally or vertically along the endpoint of another line, a horizontal or vertical constraint is applied to the line. Save your changes.

093

IMPORTANT

In AutoCAD 2011 and later versions you can define setting groups and filters in the **Settings Manager.** Generally, a group of settings contains a subgroup of all the settings defined for the current space. You can open the Settings Manager from the command located in the Manage tool group, in the Parametric tab.

You cannot infer fixed, softened, mirror, concentric, equal, or co-linear constraints.

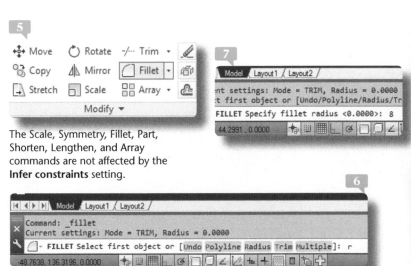

The Scale, Symmetry, Fillet, Part, Shorten, Lengthen, and Array commands are not affected by the **Infer constraints** setting.

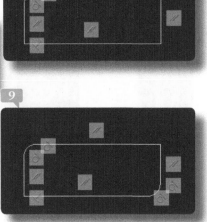

Working with graphic windows

AUTOCAD ALLOWS YOU TO VIEW A DRAWING from different angles, allowing greater precision when handling and modifying it.

1. In this exercise you will learn how to work with graphic windows. Open the **Windows.dwg** drawing, which you can download from our website. Starting with AutoCAD 2012 the program has a **View** tab, on the upper left corner of the work area, which allows you to configure the view of the entire work window and enable different view tools, customize viewpoints, manage views and select and manage visual styles. Click on the – sign in the View tab.

2. To display the drawing in different windows, in the menu of this tab, click on the **Viewport Configuration List** option and choose the **Four: Equal** option.

3. As you can see, AutoCAD has several default configurations that allow you to divide the graphic zone into 2, 3, or 4 windows in which the drawing is displayed from the same angle by default. Select the upper right window, open the **Viewport Configuration List** and, in this case, choose the **Single** option.

The View tab only appears in the Model space.

1

[−][Top][Wireframe]

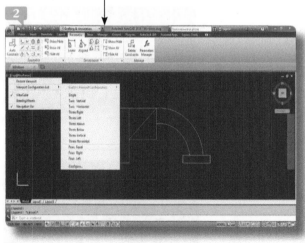

2

You can also access the settings list for graphic windows from the **Graphic windows** group in the View tab.

094

4. To open the **Viewport Configuration List** dialog box, click on the tab with the – again, click on the **Viewport Configuration List** option, and choose **Configure**.

5. In the **New Viewpoints** tab in the **Viewpoints** dialog box, a list is displayed with all the type of multiple windows included in AutoCAD. Click on the **Four: Equal** option in the **Standard viewpoints** section.

6. With the **2D** configuration, the windows in which you divide the work area will always display the current view of the drawing. Click on the arrow button in the **Setup** field and choose the **3D** option.

7. Configure this option so the lower right window displays the current view instead of the upper one. In the **Preview** section, select the window that looks like the **Top** view, click on the Change view to menu, and choose the **Current** option.

8. Apply a name to the new settings so they are saved and you can use them whenever you want. Type **Test** in the **New name** dialog box and click on the **OK** button so that the four graphic windows appear on screen.

9. Notice that, when selecting an object in any of these windows, it is also selected in the others. Draw a selection box that includes the entire object in the lower right window.

10. Press the **Escape** key to unselect the object and finish the exercise by saving your changes.

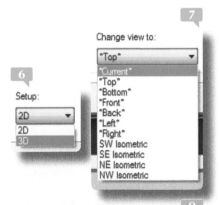

Change view to:

"Top"

"Current"
"Top"
"Bottom"
"Front"
"Back"
"Left"
"Right"
SW Isometric
SE Isometric
NE Isometric
NW Isometric

Setup:

2D

2D
3D

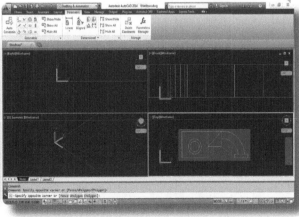

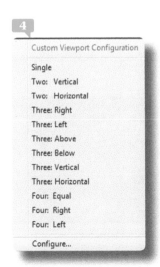

Custom Viewport Configuration

Single
Two: Vertical
Two: Horizontal
Three: Right
Three: Left
Three: Above
Three: Below
Three: Vertical
Three: Horizontal
Four: Equal
Four: Right
Four: Left
Configure...

Standard viewports:

"Active Model Configuration"
Single
Two: Vertical
Two: Horizontal
Three: Right
Three: Left
Three: Above
Three: Below
Three: Vertical
Three: Horizontal
Four: Equal
Four: Right
Four: Left

New name: Test

Applying different views to graphic windows

VIEWS ARE GRAPHICAL REPRESENTATIONS of a drawing from a point of view specified by you, displayed on screen or in graphic windows.

1. In this exercise you will learn how to apply different views to graphic windows and to modify some of their settings. To begin, click on any point of the upper left graphic window in the **Windows.dwg** example file.

2. Click on the second view tag, which looks like the view **Right**, and choose the **Top** view in the pop-up menu.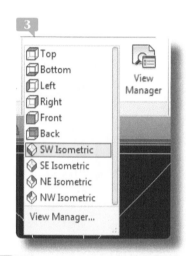

3. Notice how the look of the active graphic window changes, displaying the object in the drawing from above. Click on the graphic window to the right of the one you just modified, open the **Views** command in the **View** tab and click on the **SW Isometric** option.

4. Activate the upper left graphic window by clicking on any free point in it, open the **Views** tab again and choose the **Back** option.

5. To access the **Saved Views** function, click on the **View Manager** command in the **Views** group.

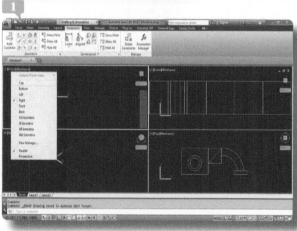

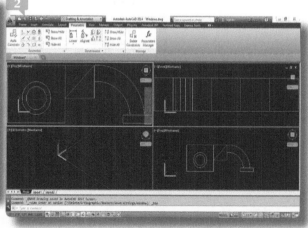

The **View Controls** is a feature that was introduced in AutoCAD 2012.

6. This opens the **View Manager** dialog box, which contains a list of available views. The first item in the list is the **Current** view, in which you will work. Select it and notice that all of its features are listed on the right, then click on the **New** button

7. Type **Test** in the **View name** field in the **New View/Shot Properties** dialog box.

8. Define a selection box that includes the zone of the drawing that will be displayed in the view you are going to save. Click on the **Define window** option in the **Boundary** section.

9. The View Manager window is temporarily hidden so that you can create the selection area in the graphic window. Type the coordinates **-2238,63** and press **Return** to locate the first corner of the selection window on this point.

10. Enter the coordinates **-2031,-22** and press the **Return** key twice.

11. Press the **OK** button in the Properties window and press the **Set Current** button while keeping the view you created selected.

12. Click on the **OK** button to apply the change and notice how the active graphic window is now displayed.

13. Finish the exercise by saving your changes.

IMPORTANT

The **VPCONTROL** system variable determines whether the Viewport Controls is displayed on the upper left corner of each graphic window with its tool, view, and visual style menus. This variable is disabled by default.

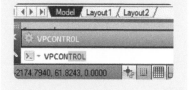

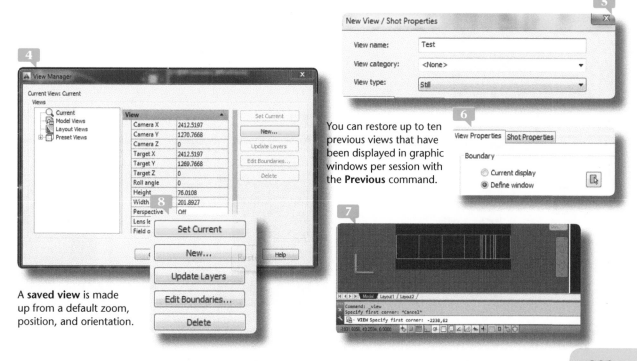

A **saved view** is made up from a default zoom, position, and orientation.

You can restore up to ten previous views that have been displayed in graphic windows per session with the **Previous** command.

Creating new custom views

IMPORTANT

To restore a previous view, use the **Back** command in the **Navigate 2D** tool group in the View tab. To go to the next view, use the **Forward** button.

AS YOU SAW IN THE PREVIOUS EXERCISE, the View Manager allows you to create, define, rename, modify, and delete saved views, including saved model views, camera views, presentation views, and default views.

1. In this exercise you will learn how to create and save a custom view so that you can reuse it whenever you need to. Activate the second viewer by clicking on it.

2. Open the **View Manager** window using the appropriate command in the **Views** group or by typing **view** in the Command Line. Press the **Return** key.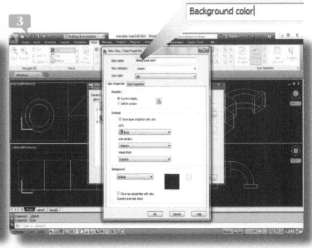

3. In the previous exercise you already created a simple new view called **Test**. In this exercise you will repeat a few steps and will customize the view further. Click on the **New** button.

4. This opens the **New View/Shot Properties** dialog box, from which you can define the area of the drawing you want to display and monitor the visual look of the objects in the view and its background. Enter **Background color** in the **View name** field.

5. Select the **Define window** option.

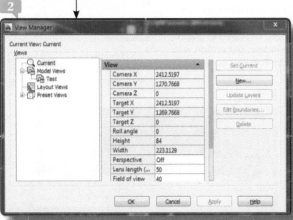

6. You now have to create a selection window in the active viewer. Type in the coordinates **662,1470** and press **Return**.

7. Type the coordinates **875,1198** for the second corner of the selection window and press the **Return** key twice.

8. In the **Settings** section, choose the visual style with which the new custom view will be saved. Keep in mind that this setting is only active in **Model** views. Open the visual style field and select the **Wireframe** option.

9. The **Background** section allows you to control the look of the background of the saved view when a 3D visual style is applied or the view is modelized. Views are created with a black background by default. Select the menu in the **Background** section and choose the **Gradient** option.

10. This opens the **Background** window that allows you to customize the gradient effect, which is made up of two colors by default. Click on the black sample, choose a blue tone in the **Select Color** window and click on the **OK** button in this window and the **Background** window.

11. Click on the **OK** button in the **New view/instant Properties** window.

12. With the new view, **Background color**, selected in the **View Manager,** click on the **Set Ccurrent** button.

13. Click on the **Apply** and **OK** buttons to apply the new view and, after seeing the effect, save your changes.

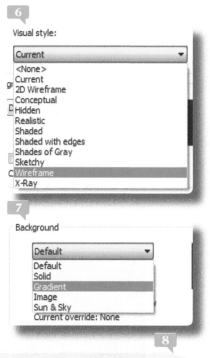

6

Visual style:

Current

<None>
Current
2D Wireframe
Conceptual
Hidden
Realistic
Shaded
Shaded with edges
Shades of Gray
Sketchy
Wireframe
X-Ray

7

Background

Default

Default
Solid
Gradient
Image
Sun & Sky
Current override: None

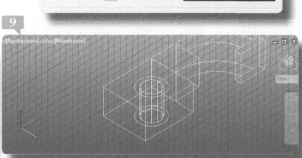

8

Gradient options

☐ Three color   Top color:

Rotation:

0   Bottom color:

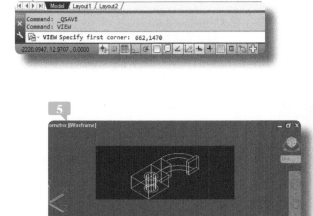

AutoCAD 2014 new file tabs

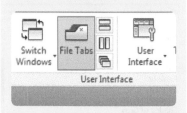
AN IMPORTANT INNOVATION IN THIS VERSION OF AUTOCAD is the introduction of new file tabs. This new feature allows you to present files in tabs, offering a more visual and faster way to work and switch between multiple open files simultaneously. In this exercise you will learn how this new tool can help you work with multiple open files.

1. Get a preview of each drawing by moving the mouse over each tab.

2. Files that are not yet saved are displayed with an asterisk.

3. Open files that are read-only are shown with a padlock.

4. An icon with the a + appears to the right of the tabs, which indicates that the tab can be used to create a new file.

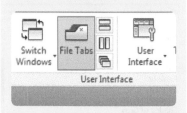

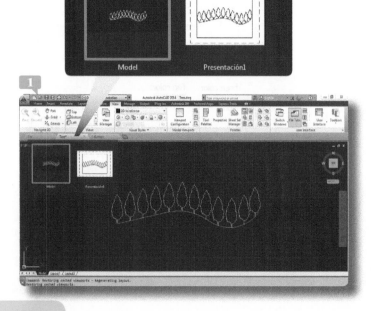

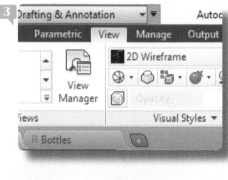

5. All the different tabs can be dragged to change their location and arrange them in a way that best suits your needs. In this example, put the **Cylinder** tab in front of the **Box** tab. 🔲

6. Each tab can be closed with the cross that appears on the right. 🔲

7. Use each tab to access a **model** space or any presentation that has been previously created. 🔲

8. When clicking the right mouse button on any of these tabs, a number of options such as opening a new file, opening an existing file, saving a file, or closing a file appears. Highlight the option that allows you to close all open files/tabs other than the current file and the one called **Open File Location** which opens the **File browser** for the folder where the file in question is located. 🔲

9. Direct printing is possible from these tabs as well. 🔲

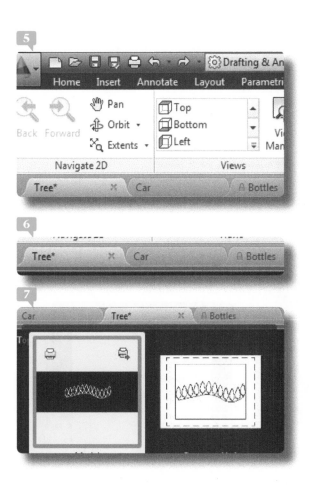

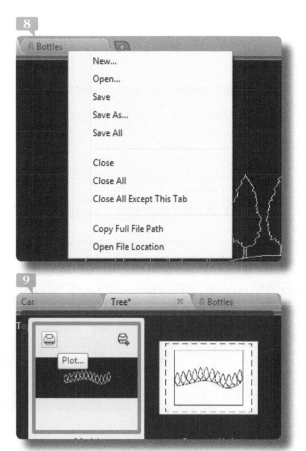

More AutoCAD 2014 new features

DUE TO THE NUMBER OF SMALL NEW FEATURES in Auto-CAD 2014 this exercise will show you how to use some of these new features.

1. The Command Line has more search options, including **Automatic Correction,** 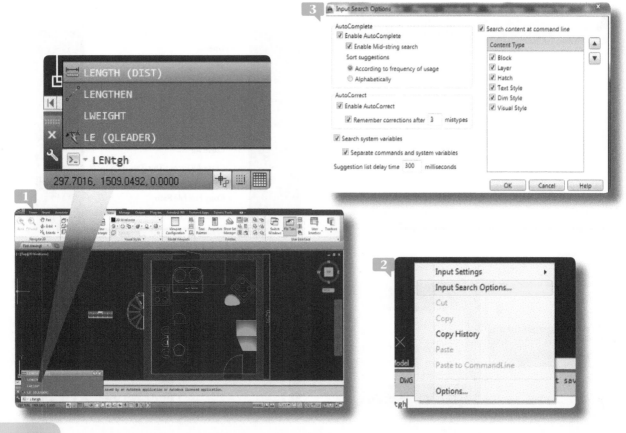 which will automatically correct any typing error. If you mix up some letters when typing a command, the program will offer you the correct word.

2. Another improvement in the Command Line is the **Search for synonyms**, which appear in parentheses next to the actual command.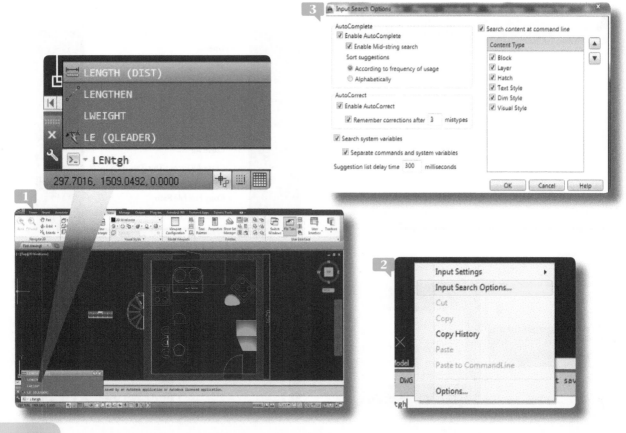

3. To customize the search function, right-click on the Command Line and select **Input Search Options.** The corre-

sponding menu opens, which allows you to enable or disable **AutoComplete** and **AutoCorrect** functions while typing an command. It also allows you to look for system variables.

4. On the right-hand side of the menu you can select the **Content** that you can search for in the Command Line. To see an example, click on the **Cancel** option and type **Ansi** in the Command Line , select one of the proposed shading options. You can Click directly on the table to apply the hatch.

5. Repeat the operation by typing **stove** in the Command Line. Select **counter block** and click directly to the left of the drawing to insert this block.

6. Finish the exercise by saving your changes.

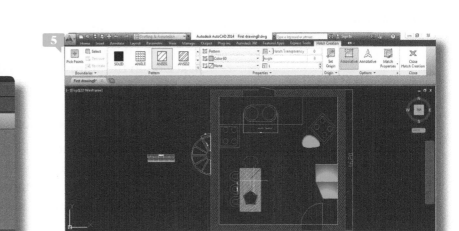

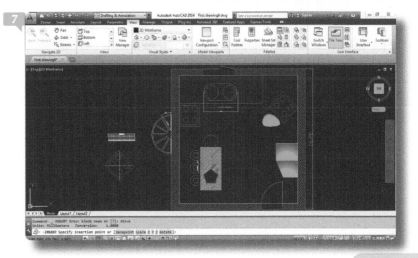

Model space and Paper space

THERE ARE TWO WorkspaceS, as you have seen, in which you can create objects: the Model space and the Paper space. The Model space is the 3D interface in which geometric objects are created on a 1:1 scale, whereas the 2D Paper space is reserved for the final presentation, specific views, and annotations for the drawing.

1. In this exercise you will practice with different presentations of the **First drawing9.dwg** file. In order to switch to the **Paper** space, click on the **Model** command on the right of the **Status Bar.**

2. Notice that the active tab under the graphic zone, at this moment, is the one called **Presentation1** and the command you clicked on in the **Status Bar** now displays the word **Paper**. By applying an **Extents** zoom you will notice that the outer limits of the white rectangle are surrounded by another rectangle, with discontinuous lines, which represents the print area.

3. You can only select and edit objects specific to the **Paper** space, such as graphic windows or text boxes, from a presentation tab. You must return to the **Model** space to edit any other objects. As an example, try to select the table; notice how the

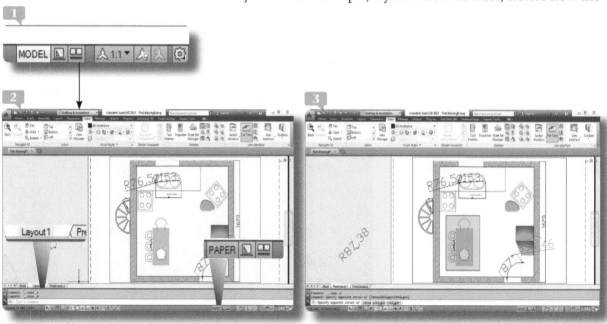

only thing you can do is draw a window. Press the **Escape** key to cancel the action.

4. Return to the **Model** space. To do this, use the quick presentation views. Click on the command on the right of the one called **Paper**, which corresponds to the **Presentation quick view** option, in the **Status Bar.**

5. This displays all the existing presentations as miniatures. Click on the Model miniature. This takes you automatically back to the **Model** space.

6. The program launches with two presentation fields, called **Presentation1** and **Presentation2**, by default. However, you can change their names, add or delete presentations, move them or copy them, etc. All these actions are found in the pop-up menus of the commands themselves, or, if you use a quick presentation view, by using the different commands for the miniatures. See, for instance, how to change the name of the **Presentation2** tab. As the miniatures are still active, double-click on the name of **Presentation2**.

7. The name **Presentation2** is highlighted in blue, which means it is in Edit mode. Type **Modified** and press **Enter.**

8. To finish, back in the **First drawing9.dwg** file, go to the **Model** space and click on the **Save** command in the **Quick Access Toolbar.**

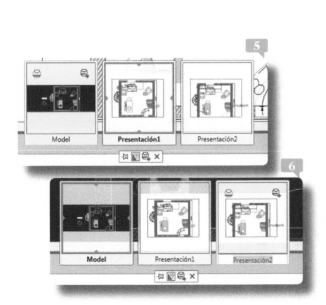

Plotting (printing)

IMPORTANT

The **Plot** dialog box, which you can open by clicking on the **Plot** command in the tool group in the **Exit** tab, or from the **Quick Access Toolbar** by clicking on the **Plot** option in the Print command in the Application menu, or by typing **plot + Return** in the **Command Line**, contains a large number of options and settings for printing.

AUTOCAD ALLOWS YOU TO PRINT DRAWINGS with different devices: conventional printers or large printers, also known as plotters. In this exercise you will learn how to print a drawing in AutoCAD.

1. Use the **First drawing9.dwg** file. In order to configure printing options you need to go to the **Plot** window. To do this, click on the **Output** tab in the **Options Ribbon** and click on the first command in the **Plot** tool group.

2. The **Plot - Model** window opens, with the necessary options to configure the printing settings.

3. Click on the arrow button in the **Name** field in the **Printer/plotter** section, and choose your printer from the drop-down menu. In order to access the properties of the selected printer, click on the **Properties** button next to its name.

4. This opens the **Plotter Configuration Editor** dialog box, which allows you to change the current configuration parameters for your installed printer. Click on the **Modify Standard Paper Sizes** (Printable Area) option that appears in the top

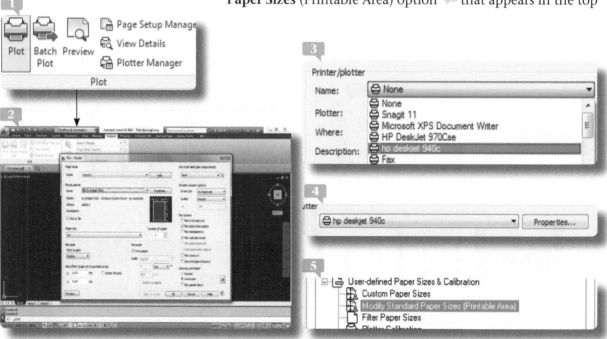

window of the **Plotter Configuration Editor**. Use the scroll bar to browse and select the **A4** option. Click on **OK** to close the window.

5. You can specify the amount of copies you want in the **Number of copies** section of the **Plot - Model** window. In this case, keep the option 1.

6. The **Plot area** section allows you to specify the part of the drawing that you want to print. In this example, print the zone with the table exclusively. Click on the arrow button in the **What to plot** field and choose the **Window** option.

7. The program returns to the presentation and allows you to draw the window that will limit the print area in the drawing, in this case, the table.

8. The **Plot scale** section controls the relative size of drawing units compared to plotted units.

9. In order to see a preview of what the presentation will look like on paper, click on the **Preview** button. The program displays a complete view of the drawing as it will appear on paper. Press the **Return** key to return to the **Plot - Model** window.

10. Click on the **Apply to Layout** button to save the changes in the current presentation.

11. Once you have defined all the print settings, and if your printer is correctly configured and connected, click on the OK button to close the **Plot - Model** window and print the drawing.

IMPORTANT

The terms **print** and **plot** are practically synonymous in **AutoCAD**. In fact, in versions prior to **AutoCAD 2010**, all print commands were called Print, whereas they were renamed to Plot in the 2010 version. The difficulty of moving a drawing to paper depends on whether the printer connected to your computer is prepared to print **AutoCAD** drawings and if the program has been correctly configured to work with it.

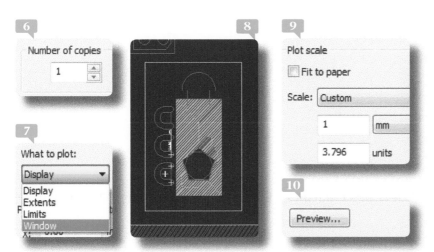

6
Number of copies
1

7
What to plot:
Display
  Display
  Extents
  Limits
  Window

8

9
Plot scale
☐ Fit to paper
Scale: Custom
  1   mm
  3.796   units

10
Preview...

12
Apply to Layout

13
OK

To continue learning ...

IF THIS BOOK HAS MET YOUR EXPECTATIONS

This book is part of a collection that covers the most commonly used and known software in all professional areas.

All books in the series have the same approach as the one that you have just finished. So, if you would like to know more about the new features of Office 2013 or other software packages, on the next page you will find other books in this collection.

MARCOMBO, Gran Via de les Corts Catalanes, 594, 08007 Barcelona - Tel. 933 180 079

PHOTO EDITING

If you want to know all the secrets of the most widely used and popular program for editing images, Learning Photoshop CS6 with 100 Practical Exercises is undoubtedly the book you are looking for.

Photoshop is the preeminent program for photo editing and image processing. With this manual you will learn how to take advantage of its many tools and functions. In this new CS6 version of Photoshop, which is the subject of this book, Adobe has included interesting and groundbreaking developments that improve and facilitate the flow of work and increase image editing possibilities.

Using this book:

- You will get to know the new Crop in Perspective Tool.
- You will retouch images with incredible features such as Fill According to Content and the new Content-Aware Patch Tool.
- You will freely transform certain parts of an image.
- You will work on a new and spectacular 3D interface to achieve the best 3D effects.

COMPUTER-AIDED DESIGN

If you want to know all the secrets of design in one of the most valued programs out right now, Learning Illustrator CS6 with 100 Practical Exercises is undoubtedly the book you are looking for.

Illustrator the vector drawing application from Adobe, is an excellent tool for computer-aided design. Thanks to its amazing and powerful features, you can create original artwork using drawings and images. Use the 100 exercises in this book to expand your knowledge and discover the thousand and one possibilities hidden in this great program.

Using this book:

- Learn about the enhanced tools for creating patterns.
- Discover the improved image tracing tool that now provides clean lines and a perfect fit.
- Apply gradients on strokes to get interesting and striking results.

OPERATING SYSTEMS

If you want to know all the secrets of the most widely used operating system, Learning Windows 8 with 100 Practical Exercises is undoubtedly the book you are looking for.

Windows 8 is Microsoft's new version of its operating system loaded with many new functions. You'll see the changes that Microsoft has made as soon as you start your session: A new customizable start screen that displays icons that can access the programs and applications installed on your computer. The new Metro interface of Windows 8 is specially designed to work with touch-screen devices.

Using this book:

- Get to know the Metro interface of Windows 8.
- Practice with the Ribbon in Windows Explorer.
- Work with the new and advanced Task Manager.
- Learn how to use new security and maintenance tools to always keep your PC as safe as possible.

IMAGE RETOUCH

If you want to improve the appearance of your digital photos and create amazing compositions, Learning Image Retouch with Photoshop CS6 with 100 Practical Exercises is undoubtedly the book you are looking for.

Photoshop is the preeminent program for retouching photographs and image processing. With the help of this manual you will learn how to use the different tools, filters, and functions in order to improve the appearance of your digital photos and create amazing compositions.

Using this book:

- Learn how to correct typical defects in photographs taken by inexperienced photographers (overexposure, underexposure, blurs, keystoning, etc.).
- Discover simple but extraordinary techniques to retouch small defects in portraits of people (dark circles, flaws, wrinkles, etc.).